CYRENIUS H. BOOTH LIBRARY

RANDOM
HOUSE
LARGE
PRINT

Grow Younger, Live Longer

Also by Deepak Chopra available
from Random House Large Print

How to Know God

Grow Younger, Live Longer

10 Steps to Reverse Aging

Deepak Chopra, M.D.,
and David Simon, M.D.

RANDOM HOUSE
LARGE PRINT

Published in the United States of America by Random House Large Print in association with Harmony Books, New York and simultaneously in Canada by Random House of Canada Limited, Toronto.
Distributed by Random House, Inc., New York.

Grateful acknowledgment is made to the following for permission to use previously published material:
Daniel Ladinsky: Lines from *I Heard God Laughing—Renderings of Hafiz,* copyright 1996 by Daniel Ladinsky.
Published by Sufism Reoriented, Walnut Creek, CA.

The Library of Congress has established a cataloging-in-publication record for this title.
ISBN 0-375-43123-3

FIRST LARGE PRINT EDITION

This Large Print edition published in accord with the standards of the N.A.V.H.

Acknowledgments

There are many souls contributing to the collective dream that is transforming our vision of health, aging, and life itself. To each of you who remind us on a regular basis of our essential purpose and meaning, we thank you from the depths of our being.

In particular we wish to acknowledge: Carolyn Rangel, Nan Johnson, Jennifer Pugh, Nicolette Martin, Jenny Hatheway, Roger Gabriel, Dennis Sugioka, Jude Hedlund, Sara Kelly, Veronique Franceus, Brent Becvar, Chantal Kovatch, Debbie Myers, and the team of immeasurably nurturing and talented people at the Chopra Center for Well Being and MyPotential.

Leanne Backer, for developing our age-reversing menu and for her power to transform love into food.

Peter Guzzardi, our beloved editor, who continuously encourages us to push the envelope.

We would also like to acknowledge the love and support of our families, which enable us to do our work: Rita Chopra, Mallika Chopra, Sumant Mandal, Gautam Chopra, Pamela Simon, Max Simon, and Sara Simon.

Contents

Grow Younger, Live Longer

Introduction

In 1993, the first edition of *Ageless Body, Timeless Mind: The Quantum Alternative to Growing Old* was released. The essential message of the book was that the human body is not a piece of biological machinery that deteriorates steadily and inexorably over time. Rather, human beings are magnificently organized networks of energy, information, and intelligence in dynamic exchange with their environment, fully capable of transformation and renewal. Since the publication of *Ageless Body, Timeless Mind,* thousands of patients at the Chopra Center for Well Being have experienced profound changes in the quality of their lives by applying the principles presented in that book, which at this writing is in its eleventh printing. According to many readers and literary critics, *Ageless Body, Timeless Mind* remains a classic, consciousness-based approach to the reversal of aging.

Grow Younger, Live Longer: 10 Steps to Reverse

Aging extends this consciousness-based approach and includes ten practical steps that can become habit-forming, enabling you to reset your Biostat (your biological, or functional, age) up to fifteen years younger than your chronological age. We have intentionally made this new book simple and practical, so you can begin implementing these approaches right away. By integrating these insights and practices into your lifestyle, you will notice immediate improvements in your physical and emotional well-being. As you begin to reverse your biological age, you will reclaim the ability to tap into your inner reservoir of unlimited energy, creativity, and vitality. You will feel younger and you will function like a much younger person, too.

Our generation has been celebrated for its willingness to challenge the prevailing assumptions of society. Rather than viewing the second half of life as a time of progressive deterioration in body and mind, we see aging as an opportunity for greater wisdom, love, creativity, meaning, joy, and increased mental and physical capacity. More people than ever before are living into their eighties, nineties, and beyond with sound bodies and clear minds.

This book is designed as a manual for renewal.

Three very practical recommendations are suggested for each of the ten steps. Each week we encourage you to implement the action steps so that by the end of ten weeks you are taking full advantage of all the resources available to you. Although awareness is the essential first step in any transformation, unfortunately, *reading* this book is not enough for you to begin reversing the aging process—you have to actually *execute* the recommendations on a daily basis in order to reap the benefits of this program.

Readers familiar with our previous works may ask if it really matters that we reverse our aging. If, as we often state, we are immortal souls on an eternal cosmic highway without beginning or end, if our essential nature is transcendental reality not subject to the laws of the material world, does it really matter if we grow younger and live longer? Why should we care about maintaining a youthful appearance for an extended time? Is it mere vanity? Does it take our attention away from our true self?

To those of you who ask these questions, we answer that in the deeper reality, all is play. Life is a cosmic game of hide and seek in which we lose ourselves to find ourselves. At our core we are all members of the same being and it does not matter if we are young or old, villain or hero, sinner or saint. The real purpose of the book is to remind you, the reader, that this deeper reality, the domain of pure potentiality, of spirit, is the essence of who you really are. Reversing aging and growing younger is part of the possibility. Whether you choose to activate this choice and implement this possibility is up to you.

We believe our primary purpose here is to seek the pure spiritual potential that is available to all of us. As human beings, the vehicles we use to explore our spiritual potential are the human body, the human nervous system, and the human mind. We therefore believe it is worth focusing attention on maintaining optimal functioning of our body/mind so we can seek our true nature as spiritual beings.

The experience of life through a human nervous system is a miraculous gift of creation. We are blessed among species in that we can change our perceptions, interpretations, and expectations of life and thereby transform our reality. As a result of changing our perceptions and taking new action steps, we can literally create a different physical body. As an expression from the ancient Ayurvedic system of healing tells us, *To know a person's experiences from the past, examine their body now. To know a person's body in the future, examine their experiences now.*

The basis of these principles and of this book

is that every impulse of experience is transformed into the chemistry and electricity of your body. With every thought, sensation, and feeling you have, your nervous system undergoes subtle shifts in physiology, generating chemical messengers that regulate your body. These biochemical communicators continuously mold the molecules that comprise your cells, tissues, and organs.

The field of mind/body medicine declares that you can influence your health and well-being through the choices you make. Your mind and body are intimately interwoven so that changes in one instantaneously influence the other. Our personal and professional experience at the Chopra Center makes us confident that applying the principles and practices offered in this program will enhance the way you think and the way you feel. You have the capacity to reverse your aging. This book provides the tools. We welcome you on this journey to renewal and look forward to hearing about your success.

How to Use This Book

Human aging is reversible. Read this book at least twice and make sure you understand all the principles. If something is not clear to you, send an e-mail to younger@chopra.com. Once you feel confident that you have grasped the essence of this book, set a date for fully committing to the ten-step program. Make the ten steps a routine for ten weeks. You will be amazed at the results.

Ten weeks is about the time it takes to create a habit. Congratulations. You are on your way to looking, feeling, and being young as a lifelong habit.

1

Escaping the Prison of Conditioning

The "normal" experience of the body and its aging is a conditioned response— a habit of thinking and behavior. By changing your habits of thinking and behavior, you can change the experience of your body and its aging.

You have been living inside a prison that has no visible walls—the confines of your self derive entirely from the habits and conditioning of your mind. If you are committed to growing younger, you must escape this prison of conditioning. You are not to blame for living within unnecessary limitations. If a rope is tied around the leg of a baby elephant and attached to a stake in the ground, it learns that it can move only within very narrow limits. Years later, as a powerful adult, it still remains within narrow confines when its leg is staked, even though it has the strength to uproot an entire tree. It has been conditioned to accept the limitations imposed upon it.

In a similar way, most people think and act within the narrow limitations of what they have been taught during childhood, without questioning the basic assumptions that structure their worldview. To live a healthier, richer, more creative life you need to recognize that most of what you hold to be true derives from habits of thought. We are born into a prevailing conversation about the world. As soon as we are capable of speaking, we engage in this conversation, reinforcing with our own thoughts and actions the patterns of thinking and behavior that surround us. This is unmistakably true in regards to how we view the body and its aging.

Until recently, few have questioned the assumption that aging is irreversible, and therefore, for generation after generation, people have reinforced the habitual thinking that growing older meant a progressive decline in mental and physical capacity. It is now time to change our habits of thinking and behaving and alter our experience of the body and the aging process.

The Quantum Possibilities

Drawing upon the wisdom traditions of the East, the dramatic new discoveries of modern quantum physics, and our own personal and professional experience, we invite you to change the way you think about and experience the world and your body. Despite how radical some of these ideas may at first appear, we encourage you to try out the practical approaches we offer and experience for yourself how this program can revitalize your body and mind.

From the perspective of quantum physics, reality is a mysterious, magical place. While on the physical plane of everyday life, time and space predominate and entropy, decay, and aging are the normal course of events, these are not features of quantum reality. The quantum realm is the fountainhead of pure potentiality, giving rise to the raw material of your body, your mind, and the physical universe. The quantum realm is the womb of creation, the invisible world where the visible is designed and assembled. We can summarize the key principles of quantum physics in five main points:

1. In the quantum realm there are no fixed objects, only possibilities.
2. In the quantum realm, everything is interwoven and inseparably one.
3. Quantum leaps are a feature of the quantum realm. A quantum leap is the ability to move from one location in space or time to another without having to go through any place or time in between.
4. One of the laws of the quantum realm is the Uncertainty Principle, which states that an event is a particle (matter) and a wave (energy) simultaneously. Your intention determines whether you see a particle or a wave.
5. In the quantum realm, an observer is needed to create an event. Before a subatomic parti-

cle is observed, it exists only as a virtual particle; all events are virtual events until the moment they are observed.

Your own body/mind system is also an expression of the same quantum field that underlies everything in the universe. Therefore, you can apply these quantum principles to the way you look at your body and aging. Rephrased in terms of your biology, they would be:

1. You are not merely the physical body that you identify with out of habit. Your essential state is a field of infinite possibilities.
2. Your body is inseparably one with the whole universe. When you are perfectly healthy or whole, you feel expanded. You become constricted only when you have discomfort or dis-ease. This comes from a feeling of separation.
3. You are capable of taking quantum leaps in perception and interpretation. With these quantum leaps you can alter not only the experience of the physical body but its very structure. Your physical body is capable of taking a quantum leap from one biological age to another without having to go through all the intervening ages in between.
4. Your body is simultaneously material (parti-

clelike) and non-material (wavelike). You can choose to experience your body as physical or as a network of energy, transformation, and intelligence.

5. Before you decide which biological age you choose to experience, you are all possible biological ages. It's up to you to decide what age you want to be.

If you choose to see yourself as a physical entity, separate from everything else, you discard the chance to reverse the aging process. If you are able to look at yourself as a field of possibilities, intimately interrelated to everything else, wonderful new opportunities emerge. We encourage you to use these thoughts to trigger a paradigm shift in your awareness. With this shift you can gain a completely different understanding of the body/mind system you inhabit, the world you perceive, and the essence of your being.

Viewing your body from the perspective of quantum physics opens up new modes of understanding and experiencing the body and its aging.
The practical essence of this new understanding is that human beings can reverse their aging.

In the Language of Spirit

Knowledge traditions seek to understand and explain the workings of the cosmos. The perspective of quantum physics offers a fascinating way to view life, the body, and aging. The perennial wisdom traditions of the East offer equally amazing insights into the nature of reality. As explorers of both modern science and the ancient knowledge traditions, we are enthused and inspired by the closer and closer alignment between these different perspectives on life. According to Ayurveda, the ancient healing tradition of India, aging is an illusion because your true self is neither your body nor your mind. Your essential nature, *who you really are,* is the domain of ever-present witnessing awareness that is beyond your physical and mental layers. This field of consciousness gives rise to both the thoughts in your mind and the molecules in your body. Tapping into this realm of awareness where time and space have no meaning is the basis of emotional and physical renewal.

Accessing this field of pure potentiality has spiritual as well as physical consequences. Knowing your essential self as a nonlocal being, inextricably interrelated to everything else in the cosmos, awakens greater creativity, meaning, and purpose in life. Although the most profound way to improve health and reverse aging is ultimately a spiritual one, not everyone is immediately ready to accept this approach. One person may want to lose weight, another may need help to stop smoking, while a third may be seeking a more fulfilling love relationship. Each of these needs is important in its own right, but taking a spiritual approach opens the door to the evolution of consciousness, which can make all these things possible, and many more.

A spiritual approach means that we expand
our awareness,
even while focusing our attention and
intention locally.

The reason we perform any action is in the hope that it will bring us satisfaction, fulfillment, and happiness. Embracing the spiritual domain, which is the source and goal of all desires in life, creates the possibility for satisfaction, happiness, and fulfillment independent of the inevitably changing situations, circumstances, and people that surround us. Those fortunate ones who dwell in this domain have achieved what is often called enlightenment.

Viewing your choices from a spiritual perspective means asking the big questions: Who are you? Why are you here? What do you really want? How can you best serve? Although at first glance these questions may seem irrelevant to slowing the aging process, they are actually essential to renewal. Shifting your internal reference point from an egocentric being, whose sense of worth depends upon the positions and possessions one has accumulated, to a network of conscious energy, woven from the threads of universal intelligence, has a profound effect on your mind and body. When you become clear that the reason you want to live to a hundred or more years is so you can express your full creative potential, *you change your chemistry and physiology.* When you identify your unique talents and commit to using them in the service of others, *you strengthen your immune system.* When you decide that exercising regularly or preparing a balanced meal is an enjoyable experience, *you improve your circulatory health and lower your blood pressure.* Your perceptions, interpretations, and expectations influence every aspect of your mental and physical health. Shifting your perspective and making new choices provide you with powerful tools to change your life.

The Window to Renewal

One of the ways science makes major advances is by studying situations, circumstances, and events that are the exception to the usual way things work. These are sometimes called anomalies, or exceptions to the rule. Most scientists ignore anomalies, but in fact, these are the very things we should be studying. If something breaks the rule, no matter what it is, no matter how infrequent it is, no matter how remote the probability, it means that a new possibility has arisen. And if a new possibility has presented itself, there must be a mechanism. Even if only one person out of ten million cures himself of cancer or of AIDS, we have to pay attention. Most scientists tend to disregard events that are so rare they do not regularly infringe upon the prevailing view of the world. They may dismiss an anomaly by saying that it is so rare—one in ten million—what's the point of investigating it?

The point is that it doesn't matter if something happens only once in ten million, because if it has happened even once, there must be some mechanism to account for its occurrence. And if there is a mechanism, then as scientists we want to know what that mechanism is, because once we understand the mechanism, we may be able to reproduce the phenomenon.

Galileo, Copernicus, Newton, and Einstein are examples of scientists who questioned the prevailing assumptions of their time and expanded their view to include phenomena that had previously been ignored. These and other great scientists paid attention to anomalies and sought to understand the mechanism that explains them. When something doesn't fit the paradigm, doesn't fit the pattern, doesn't fit the theory, it forces us to examine the model we are using. It compels us to expand or change the theory to incorporate the exceptional situation.

A good example of this is a friend of ours who was diagnosed with AIDS over fifteen years ago. He was close to death when he made the choice to change his life. He started meditating, began eating a healthy diet, and made the commitment to eliminate toxins from his life. Fifteen years later he is feeling completely well and has undetectable levels of the HIV virus in his blood. When we first met him, he was an anomaly, but now we know many more people like him. Our theory of consciousness predicts that if we reach a critical mass of people who have the same experience, then it will become true for everyone.

We believe that these same principles apply to human aging. If we look at recent historical times we see that the average life expectancy has shifted remarkably. The average life span of a human being during the Roman Empire was twenty-eight years. The average life span of a human being born in the Western world at the beginning of the twentieth century was forty-nine years. Although in the past, high rates of infant mortality influenced human life expectancy, the fastest-growing segment of the American population today is over the age of ninety years.

A baby girl born in America today is expected to live just less than eighty years; an infant boy has a life expectancy of almost seventy-four. Historically, there are many people who have lived to ripe old ages and have made major contributions to civilization. Leonardo da Vinci was drawing sketches in his sixties, Leo Tolstoy was writing novels into his seventies, and Michelangelo was sculpting in his eighties. Winston Churchill, with his fondness for cigars and Scotch, was active and productive until his death at age ninety. As our collective consciousness embraces the belief that we can have the biology of youth with the wisdom of experience, it will become the pervasive experience.

The Science of Aging

Recognizing that human beings do not age at the same rate, scientists have described three different ways to characterize a person's age. The first is *chronological age,* which is what your birth certificate says. Your chronological age measures the number of rotations Earth has performed on its axis and around the sun since you left your mother's womb. Your chronological age cannot be altered through mind/body approaches, but it has the least relevance to how you feel or function.

Biological age is a measurement of how well your physiological systems are functioning. It is the most important component of the aging process. Your biological age is calculated in reference to an average population of people who have the same chronological age that you have. Values for almost every biochemical and physiological process can be determined for different age groups. Known as the biological markers, or *biomarkers,* of aging, these include blood pressure, amount of body fat, auditory and visual thresholds, hormonal levels, immune function, temperature regulation, bone density, skin thickness, cholesterol levels, blood sugar tolerance, aerobic capacity, and metabolic rate (see the table on page 24). Once you know your results, you can compare them with the group average and see if your biomarkers are older or younger than your chronological peers. Your biological age can be very different from your chronological age. A fifty-year-old who takes good care of herself can have the biology of a thirty-five-year-old. Alternatively, a fifty-year-old who has not been attentive to his health may have the biology of men many years older. Whatever your biological age is today, we believe we can alter it by implementing the changes recommended in this book.

Biological age is the key component of the aging process.

Psychological age is your subjective experience of how old you feel. We meet many people in their sixties who report that they feel better than they did in their thirties. In prior times they may have been smoking two packs of cigarettes a day, were unhappy in their jobs, and were not eating well. Since instituting the ten steps to reverse aging, their mental and physical well-being has dramatically improved. They have learned to relax and enjoy life, so although they are chronologically older, they unequivocally feel younger than they did years ago. Psychological age is closely linked to biological age. When the body is functioning in a more efficient, energetic manner, we experience this vitality as feeling more alive.

Although we cannot reverse our chronological age, we *can* reverse the more important measures of our biological and psychological age—and by so doing can regain the physical and emotional vitality we had in the past.

The Biomarkers of Aging

AEROBIC CAPACITY

ANTIOXIDANT LEVELS

AUDITORY THRESHOLD

BLOOD PRESSURE

BLOOD SUGAR REGULATION

BODY FAT

BONE DENSITY

CHOLESTEROL AND LIPID LEVELS

HORMONAL LEVELS

IMMUNE FUNCTION

METABOLIC ACTIVITY

MUSCLE MASS

MUSCLE STRENGTH

SKIN THICKNESS

TEMPERATURE REGULATION

VISUAL THRESHOLD

Research into Aging

In the 1970s, Alexander Leaf, a Harvard doctor, journeyed around the world seeking the secret to a long, healthy life. He visited communities in the southern republics of the former Soviet Union, northern Pakistan, and the Andes Mountains of Ecuador, where it was rumored that many people were living dynamic, vital lives well into their eighties, nineties, and beyond. In many cases, these stories were true. Leaf discovered that the one consistent feature of these people living in widely separated regions of the world was their attitude about aging. Simply stated, in these societies, growing older meant growing better; vibrant centenarians were revered for their knowledge, physical vitality, and personal presence. They had the wisdom of experience with the biology of youth.

Another interesting study was performed by Harvard psychologist Ellen Langer. She took groups of men in their seventies and eighties and encouraged them to think and behave as if they were twenty years younger. After doing this for only five days, these men showed a number of physical changes associated with age reversal. Their hearing and vision improved, they performed better on tests of manual dexterity, and had improved joint mobility.

Both of these studies tell us the same thing. Expectations determine outcomes. If you expect your mental and physical capacity to diminish with age, it probably will. If you have the expectations that you can grow younger and live longer, this will be your experience. As more and more people shift their expectations and experience reversal of aging for themselves, it will become the expectation of everyone.

Restoring Your Life Energy

When a doctor wants to check the status of a specific biochemical in your body, he draws blood for analysis. The results obtained from scrutinizing a minute sampling are accepted as being true for the entire body. For example, if we want to check your blood sugar level, we need to examine only a minuscule amount that can be collected from a tiny pinprick. We assume that what is true for one drop of blood is true for every drop in your body. This assumption is a result of the recognition that the body is holographic. This means that the whole is contained in every part; whenever one aspect changes, everything changes.

Applying this principle to the reversal of aging, you can see that making a healthy shift in any one component of your life will have a positive influence on your entire state of well-being. The more you are able to replace life-damaging choices with life-affirming ones, the more profound the benefits you will experience physically, emotionally, and spiritually. When you reverse one biological marker of aging, you will reverse almost all the others. For example, improving your muscle strength leads to an increase in bone density. Improving your aerobic capacity enhances your immune function. Our ten-steps-to-reverse-aging program is therefore a practical holistic approach to creating a profoundly better quality of life. These approaches are simple yet powerful and we are enthusiastic to share them with you.

The body is holographic; therefore,
when you change one biomarker
you influence them all.

The conditioning of our society leads us to believe that as we grow older, we deteriorate physically and mentally. When you break out of this conditioning, you will learn from your own experience that every day in every way you can increase your physical and mental capacity. That is the promise of this book. If you practice the ten steps you will reverse your biological age, and biological age is the only age that really matters.

2

You Can Reverse Your Biological Age by Changing Your Perceptions

ACTION STEP #1

I am reversing my biological age by changing my perceptions of my body, its aging, and of time.

I put this into practice by:

1. *Changing my perception of aging by resetting my Biostat and practicing on a daily basis the rituals that remind me of my biological set point.*
2. *Changing my perception of time by the practice of self-referral techniques, bringing my attention to the nonchanging factor in the midst of change.*
3. *Changing my perception of my body by learning to experience it as a field of energy, transformation, and intelligence, practicing the Energy, Transformation, and Intelligence technique.*

Perceptions create reality.
By changing your perceptions
you change your reality.
By changing the perception
of your body, its aging, and of time,
you can reverse your biological age.

A basic principle of Ayurveda is stated as: What you see you become. What you see is a selective act of attention and interpretation. Although you are inundated by billions of bits of sensory impulses every moment, you selectively filter out the vast majority, allowing only a very small fraction into your awareness. What you allow into your awareness is determined by your habitual patterns of seeing and interpreting the world.

To make this point clear, consider a situation in which you and your friend are sitting on a park bench. Across the street a woman is walking her beagle. Your friend, the manager of a woman's apparel store, hones in on what the woman is wearing, scrutinizing her outfit. Deciding that she does not like what the woman is wearing, your friend feels mildly annoyed. As an animal lover, you barely notice the woman but instead focus on her dog, which reminds you of a puppy you had as a child, and as a result, you feel a little wistful. What is the reality? It is clearly different for both of you as a result of your selective acts of *attention* and *interpretation*.

Reality is flexible and subject to revision.
Reality is the result of perception,
which is a selective act of attention
and interpretation.

There are many visual examples of this principle. Each of the four pictures that follow demonstrates how your attention and interpretation determine your reality. The sensory data does not change when you make the leap from one interpretation to another. What you see changes as a result of a change in your consciousness.

Can you see the chalice? Can you see the faces?

Can you see the old woman? Can you see the young woman?

Do you see the face? Do you see the word?

Do you see the bird? Do you see the rabbit?

Your attention and interpretations create what you see and ultimately determine what you believe. A belief is simply an interpretation that you hold to be true. For example, due to habits of perception, most people half a millennium ago believed that the sun revolved around Earth. When Copernicus suggested that our planet was not the center of the universe, people were upset because challenging prevailing beliefs inevitably generates resistance. However, new ideas that expand awareness, enhance life, and take us closer to truth are contagious. Before long, a critical mass of people embrace the new idea, and their beliefs about themselves and the world are forever changed.

As we enter the new millennium, the insights of our most advanced scientists are just beginning to influence our collective views. Our ideas about the human body, its aging, and even time itself are undergoing a dramatic shift, opening the possibility for unprecedented health, vitality, and longevity. Let's look at how we may begin to embrace these more expanded and empowering beliefs.

Your habits of attention and interpretation
create deeply ingrained beliefs,
which are the interpretations you hold
to be true.
Beliefs create biology.

Change Your Perception of Aging

The only true way to measure the aging process is through the biomarkers of aging. By now you know that the biological markers of aging are reversible (see page 24 to review the biomarkers of aging). Now it is time to use the organizing power of your intention to set a clear expectation to reverse your aging. Your intentions establish your expectations, and your expectations influence outcome.

We know from many scientific studies that whatever you anticipate happening with your health is much more likely to occur. Doctors sometimes ridicule this as the placebo effect, but the placebo effect is a testimony to the power of intention. When a doctor and a patient believe in a treatment, the positive results can be as high as 100 percent, even if the treatment is later found to have no pharmacological effect. If patients with asthma are given salt water and told it will help their breathing, they will breathe more easily due to the placebo effect. Given the same salt water with the suggestion that their breathing will worsen, they experience the expected deterioration. This is called the nocebo effect. In every condition imaginable—from high blood pressure to cancer, from stomach ulcers to anginal heart pain—your expectations can make the difference between health and illness, life and death. We can summarize this principle in one line: What you believe you become.

We can use this principle to great effect. Set the intention to grow younger and live longer. Your intention is a powerful activator of your inner pharmacy. Your expectation of growing younger will lead to the reversal of your aging.

Setting Your Biostat

Close your eyes. Become aware of your breath, releasing any tension you may be holding in your body. Now, choose an age within the last fifteen years that you would like to be in biological terms. This means you would like to have the physical and mental capacity of a healthy person at that age, that you would like your biomarkers to reflect that particular age, that you would like to feel and look that particular age. As an example, let's assume you are sixty years old. Choose an age between forty-five and sixty. Let's say you choose the age of forty-nine years. This becomes your *Biostat*—your set point in consciousness. Just as a thermostat adjusts the temperature in a room to a particular set point, so, too, your Biostat will orchestrate your psychology and biology around the biological age you have chosen.

This will happen through the following mechanisms: (1) Your intention to stay at a particular Biostat will directly influence your body of energy, transformation, and intelligence. This is because intention influences your biochemistry through its infinite organizing power. This is the principle of teleology, which states that intended outcomes orchestrate the biological mechanisms to fulfill themselves. (2) Keeping your Biostat in your awareness will influence your thinking, your moods, and your behavior and reinforce your intention to maintain your biology at that set point. Once you have identified your set point, begin affirming it five times a day. We suggest practicing the following ritual upon awakening, before breakfast, before lunch, before dinner, and at bedtime. On each of these occasions close your eyes and mentally repeat to yourself each of the following phrases at least three times:

Every day in every way, I am increasing
my mental and physical capacity.
My Biostat is set at a healthy ____ years of age.
I look and feel a healthy ____ years old.

Within a few days of performing this ritual you will actually begin to think and act from the level of your Biostat. All your habits will be influenced, but even more important, your perception of your biological age and your experience of it will begin to shift. You will start to believe in your Biostat and its organizing power and your new belief will shape your new biology.

Change Your Perception of Time

To reverse the aging process you need to change your perception of time because how you perceive time regulates your biological clock. To do this, you need to ask a crucial question: What is time? In the physical world we use time to measure the flow of events in our lives. And yet we know that our experience of time is fluid.

Dreamtime, for example, is very different from waking time. When you are dreaming, many things can happen in a very short time, because in that state you have an entirely different perception of time. In the quantum realm, time obeys a different set of rules. Cause and effect are nonlinear, and events that we would normally consider "the future" are capable of influencing events in "the past." When we glimpse the realm of spirit through meditation or an awe-inspiring experience, we enter a domain that is beyond time and space. The experience of this is called timeless mind. Since mind and body are inseparable, a timeless mind is also an ageless body. When our mind comes to a standstill, time comes to a standstill and our biological clock stops.

One of the ways to define aging is to see it as the metabolism of time. Imagine for a moment that you could metabolize eternity or infinity instead of time. You would literally have an immortal body. The ancient seers of the Vedic tradition claimed that even occasional excursions into this timeless or eternal domain of consciousness could influence the biological clock and extend life by many years.

The human body and its biological functions respond to the experience of time. Your biological clock beats to your personal experience of time. To paraphrase Einstein, when asked to explain the theory of relativity in a way that was meaningful to everyday experience, he said, "If I burn myself on a hot stove, that fraction of a second seems like eternity. But if I'm with a beautiful woman, even eternity seems like one second. It's gone in a moment. It's never enough."

The experience of time is subjective. If you are always in a hurry, your biological clock speeds up. If you feel you have all the time in the world, your biological clock slows down. During meditation, when you enter into the gap between thoughts, time stops. That also happens when you're playing a game you enjoy, when you are listening to great music, when you experience the beauty in nature, and when you fall in love. Time is a subjective experience in consciousness and that subjective experience translates into a biological response in your body.

Accessing the Nonchanging Factor

Although experiences change, the one who is having the experience resides in the domain of nonchange. Even in the midst of any experience you can access the experiencer by a simple shift of your attention. Try this simple exercise: As you read these words, ask yourself, "Who is reading?" Now, look around the room in which you are sitting and while you are looking, silently ask yourself, "Who is observing?" If there is a radio playing or a conversation taking place in the next room, as you are listening to the sounds in your environment ask yourself, "Who is listening?" As you consciously make these subtle shifts in your awareness, you will recognize that the answer to each of these questions is the same. The one who is reading, the one who is observing, and the one who is listening is not restricted to any particular experience. It is not restricted to time or place. There is a silent witness within you that is the same presence that was you as a child, a teenager, an adult, and *now.* It is the essence of who you are. According to Ayurveda, this silent witness is your Spirit. When your internal reference point shifts from your experiences to the one who is experiencing, you break the barrier of time.

Practice shifting your attention to the nonchanging factor in the midst of change. You do this by asking "Who is having the experience?" and referring back to your witnessing self. This practice is called self-referral because you are shifting your attention to the "Self" of experience. When your attention is on the objects of experience, *the experience itself,* that quality of awareness is known as object-referral. A shift in attention from object-referral to self-referral is a shift from time-bound awareness (time-bound mind) to timeless awareness (timeless mind) because the Self is the timeless factor in the midst of time-bound experience.

There are other ways of experiencing timeless mind. Basically, they all involve the same principle. You go beyond your internal dialogue and experience a silent mind, which is the same thing as a timeless mind. Next time you feel emotional turbulence, immediately bring your attention to the sensations in your body and make a conscious choice to stop interpreting the emotional experience. When you have focused your attention on the bodily sensations that accompany an emotion, you have stopped all interpretation, and your mind becomes silent. You become the silent witness of the sensations in your body. In doing so, you not only stop your internal dialogue, but you also begin to dissipate the energy of the emotional turbulence.

Still another way of experiencing timeless mind is to become aware of the spaces between breaths, between the objects of perception, between movements of your body, and between your thoughts. If your attention is on any of these spaces and you are not in an interpreting mode, then you go beyond your internal dialogue and enter the timeless mind. Some people are able to immediately stop their internal dialogue simply by silently saying to themselves "Stop!" Use whatever works for you. The key is to have the ability to become a silent witness and experience the Self, even during activity. It is extremely important to have the ability to shift awareness from that which *changes* to that which *does not change.* Start practicing this by shifting your awareness to the Self or observer as described above, by feeling the body without interpretation, and by becoming aware of the spaces between objects.

When you can maintain this inner silence, inner centeredness, inner presence, even in the midst of outer activity, you will have a new relationship with time and everything you experience. Cultivating ever-present witnessing awareness in the midst of time-bound awareness will forever transform your perception of time.

Change Your Perception of Your Body

The prevailing worldview looks at the body as a material vehicle, similar to an automobile, in which parts inevitably break down until the body is no longer serviceable. Modern science and the wisdom traditions tell us this is a flawed interpretation. Your body is not merely a physical device that generates thoughts and feelings; rather, it is a network of energy, transformation, and intelligence in dynamic exchange with the world around you. With every breath you take, every mouthful of food or swallow of water you ingest, every sound you hear, sight you see, sensation you feel, and aroma you smell your body changes. Just since you began reading this paragraph you exchanged *four hundred billion trillion* atoms with your environment!

Your body looks static because the changes are taking place at a level too subtle for you to directly perceive. Scientists can calculate the turnover of matter in your body by labeling atoms with radioactive material and tracking their metabolism. Through this process we've learned that the lining of your stomach is replaced about every five days. It takes about a month for your skin to be retread. In about six weeks your liver has turned over, and within just a few months, most of the calcium and phosphorous crystals that make up your skeleton have come and gone. Every year over 98 percent of all the atoms in the human body have been exchanged. After a course of three years, you would be hard pressed to find an atom that was a part of you then, which could still be considered yours now.

To help you appreciate this idea, consider that your body is like a local branch of the public library. Although on one level the library seems to be stable, on another level it is constantly changing. Books are coming and going every day, with completely new ones added and old ones returned to the downtown facility. Particular books do not define a library; rather, it represents the site and process of this ever-changing exchange of information.

Your body is like a flame that is constantly metabolizing new material. The flammable matter and the oxygen necessary for its combustion must be continually renewed. The smoke and gases released are changing at every moment. And yet the flame appears to be nearly the same over time. The processes of creation, maintenance, and dissolution are simultaneously at work in a flame and in your body.

The Greek poet Heraclitus said you cannot point to the same river twice because new water is always flowing. Like a river, like a library, like a flame, your body may appear to be the same on the surface, but in actuality, it is constantly changing. Rather than viewing your body as a static biological machine, begin to think of it as a field of energy and intelligence, constantly renewing itself. To grow younger you must change your perception of the body, relinquishing the idea that it is a bag of flesh and bones. Begin to experience your body as the flow of vital energy, transformation, and intelligence, and you will experience the reversal of aging.

Even though the body appears
to be material, it is not.
In the deeper reality, your body is a field of
energy, transformation, and intelligence.

The Body of Energy, Transformation, and Intelligence

Everything we have said to this point can be summarized in one sentence: By cultivating the habit of thinking of your body as a field of energy, transformation, and intelligence, you will begin to experience it as a flexible, dynamic bundle of consciousness, rather than as a fixed, material thing. You will realize its wavelike nature instead of its particlelike nature. One way of doing this is through the use of daily rituals that reinforce this new interpretation.

Your body is a field of energy, at one with the energy of the cosmos, inexhaustible and constantly in motion. The Ayurvedic term for this energetic aspect of life is *Prana* (prä′-nä), which is sometimes translated as the breath of life. Likewise, your body is ever in transformation, always and eternally in dynamic relationship with the elements and forces of the universe. This is known in Ayurveda as *Tejas* (tĕ′-jäs), the internal fire of transformation. Finally, your body is the physical manifestation of universal intelligence, which is supreme, divine, and immortal. The Ayurvedic word for this is *Ojas* (ō′-jäs), the infinitely flexible, fluid expression of the physical body. To reverse the aging process, begin using the words *energy, transformation,* and *intelligence* as reinforcements to experience your body as it really is—a field of inexhaustible energy, in constant transformation, and as a physical expression of pure intelligence. If you prefer, you can use the Ayurvedic terms *Prana, Tejas,* and *Ojas* as mantras to anchor your new interpretation. As you begin to experience your body in its true form, your beliefs about it will also change, and your new beliefs will create your new biology.

EXERCISE—YOUR BODY OF LIGHT

Look at the picture below.

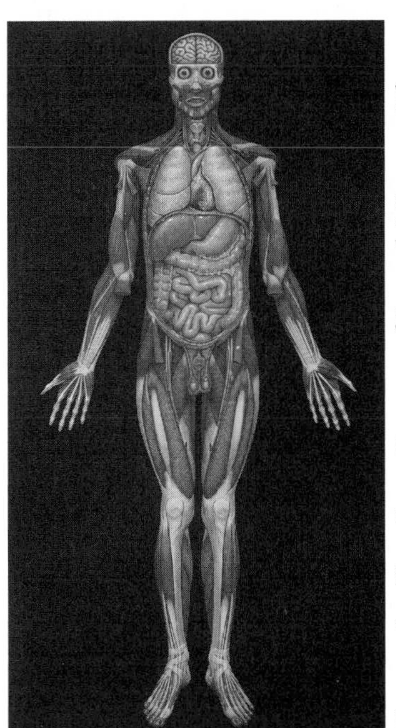

Viscera, *by Alex Grey. Courtesy of* Sacred Mirrors: The Visionary Art of Alex Grey, *Inner Traditions International. Used with permission. (www.alexgrey.com)*

Picture A

Picture A is the conventional view of the human body as a modern physician might envision it. This picture reflects how, on a subconscious level, you perceive your body at this moment. Although this perception is accurate at the gross level, it is an incomplete representation of the true nature of your body. Therefore, it is not the way you should envision your body.

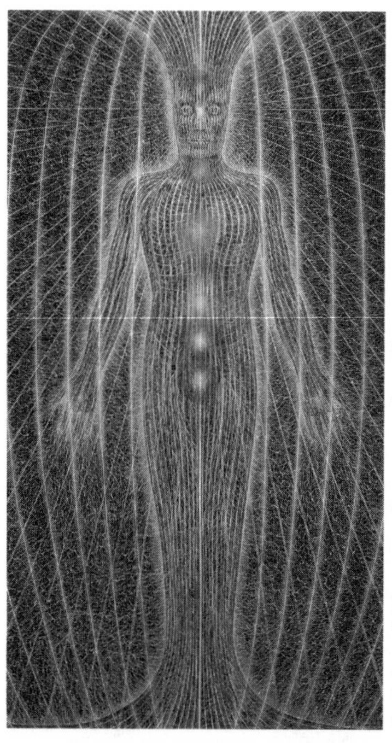

Spiritual Energy System, *by Alex Grey. Courtesy of* Sacred Mirrors: The Visionary Art of Alex Grey, *Inner Traditions International. Used with permission. (www.alexgrey.com)*

Picture B

Now look at picture B, a good representation of how your body really is at a quantum level: a field of energy, transformation, and intelligence. This is how the ancient Vedic seers saw it. They referred to it as the "subtle" body. This subtle or quantum mechanical body is inextricably woven into, and is one with, the energy and intelligence fields of the cosmos.

Look once again at picture B. Now close your eyes and see if you can clearly visualize it. Can you? Open your eyes. Look once again. Repeat this procedure as many times as you want, until you can see your subtle (quantum) body as clearly with your eyes closed as with your eyes open. When you are absolutely sure that you can do this, close your eyes again and mentally repeat to yourself: "Energy (Prana), transformation (Tejas), intelligence (Ojas)."

Whenever you consciously take a deep breath (and make it a point to do this several times each day), close your eyes and mentally repeat the word *Energy* while at the same time visualizing your energy or light body as represented in picture B. Similarly, when you consciously eat food, mentally repeat the word *Transformation,* visualizing the light body in transformation. Finally, every time you take a sip of water, silently repeat the word *Intelligence* and envision once again the light body as fluid and flexible. As you repeat this ritual with breathing, eating, and drinking, you will be starting the process of restructuring your perception and the experience of your body from material to subtle.

Perceiving Your Light Body

Enlivening Energy (Prana)

Your vital energy animates both mind and body. Throughout the day, use the word *Energy* and experience the life force rejuvenating every cell, tissue, and organ in your body.

Think "Energy" whenever you:

- Walk through a garden.
- Go from indoors to outdoors.
- Practice breathing exercises (see Chapter 7)

Enlivening Transformation (Tejas)

The essential transformational force is the primordial fire of life. Throughout the day, use the word *Transformation* to enliven the transformational process that continuously converts energy from one form into another.

Think "Transformation" whenever you:

- Take a mouthful of food.
- Feel the sun on your body
- Gaze into the stars at night.

Enlivening Intelligence (Ojas)

When intelligence is abundant and freely circulating in your body, all your physiological systems—cardiovascular, digestive, neurological, hormonal, and immune—function at their optimal level. Throughout the day, use the word *Intelligence* to enliven nourishment in every cell of your body.

Think "Intelligence" whenever you:

- Take a sip of water.
- Walk along a natural body of water.
- Drink fresh fruit juices or other healthy beverages.

In addition to silently repeating these words to enliven energy, transformation, and intelligence while you breathe, eat, and drink, use them when you are exercising. Whenever you are performing a rhythmic activity—walking, jogging, swimming, riding your bicycle, or using a treadmill—silently repeat "Energy, Transformation, Intelligence . . . Energy, Transformation, Intelligence . . ." or "Prana, Tejas, Ojas . . . Prana, Tejas, Ojas . . ." with your full attention on your body. After a while, your habitual way of experiencing your body will change because your perceptions will have shifted.

The Body as a River of Renewal

Your body is not a mechanical structure fixed in time and space. It is a field of energy, information, and intelligence in dynamic exchange with your environment, capable of perpetual healing, renewal, and transformation.

Sitting comfortably, close your eyes and take a full deep inhalation. Now, as you slowly exhale the air from your lungs, visualize your breath as a flow of molecules being released from every cell in your body. With each outgoing breath you are releasing atoms from every organ in your body, and with each ingoing breath you are bringing atoms to every cell and organ in your body. You are renewing your body and replacing parts with every breath that you take.

Continue to breathe in and out and imagine your body as a continual stream of energy and transformation, constantly renewing and refreshing itself.

Bring your attention to your stomach and know that the entire stomach lining will be renewed in less than a week. Now bring your attention to your skin and know that within one month the cells will be entirely replaced and you will have new skin.

See your skeleton in your mind's eye. The atoms that currently comprise it will be replaced by new ones in three months. Bring your attention to your liver. You will have a new one in six weeks.

Now feel your whole body. In one year almost all of it will have been replaced. Now say to yourself: "I am renewing my body with every breath I take." See your body as it really is—infinitely flexible, fluid, and forever in renewal.

Every day in every way, I am increasing
my mental and physical capacity.
My Biostat is set at a healthy ____ years of age.
I look and feel a healthy ____ years old.

I am reversing my biological age:

- *By changing my perception of my body, its aging, and time.*

3

You Can Reverse Your Biological Age Through Two Kinds of Deep Rest—Restful Awareness and Restful Sleep

ACTION STEP #2

I am reversing my biological age through two kinds of deep rest—restful awareness and restful sleep.

I put this into practice by:

1. *Experiencing restful awareness through sitting meditation with my eyes closed for a minimum of twenty minutes twice daily.*
2. *Experiencing renewal and rejuvenation every night through restful sleep.*
3. *Synchronizing my biological rhythms with the rhythms of nature.*

Agitation in body and mind
creates dis-ease and accelerates aging.
Deep rest in body and mind
reverses biological age.

Experiencing deep rest in body and mind is the next step to growing younger and living longer. An agitated body/mind system generates entropy, decay, and aging. A rested body/mind system fosters creativity, renewal, and reversal of aging. Since the body and mind are one, when the mind is deeply rested the body is also deeply rested. Of course, we know from common experience that our mind is rarely in this rested state. In fact, most of the time it is in the fight-or-flight mode. The fight-or-flight or stress response occurs when we feel threatened in any way, including when we feel threatened by aging. The stress response creates physiological changes that damage the body and accelerate aging. You are surely familiar with how it feels to be in stress mode, but you may not be familiar with what is happening in your body. The physiological changes that accompany the fight-or-flight response are:

- Your heart beats faster.
- Your blood pressure rises.
- You consume more oxygen.

- You expel more carbon dioxide.
- You breathe faster.
- Your breathing becomes shallow.
- Your heart pumps more blood.
- You sweat.
- One part of your adrenal glands pumps out adrenaline and noradrenaline, which constrict blood vessels.
- Another part of your adrenal glands pumps out cortisol.
- Your pancreas releases more of the hormone glucagon.
- Your pancreas releases less insulin.
- As a result of the increased glucagon and decreased insulin, your blood sugar level rises.
- You reduce the blood supply to your digestive organs and increase the blood supply to your muscles.
- Your pituitary gland releases less growth hormone.
- You produce lower levels of sex hormone.
- Your immune system is suppressed.

The fight-or-flight response was first described by early-twentieth-century American scientist Walter Cannon. He wanted to understand why some people became ill and others even died under stress. He discovered that when you encounter a threatening situation, a part of your involuntary nervous system becomes instantly and automatically activated. The nervous system triggers rises in blood pressure and heart rate and stimulates the adrenal glands to release adrenaline. If the threat and the neurological response are severe and unrelenting, damaging bodily changes can occur.

Cannon researched tribal societies, where people who trespass against important rules are banished from the community. A bone is pointed at the offender by the tribal witch doctor, resulting in a "curse." From that point on, the offender is no longer considered to be part of the living community. He is cut off from all social interactions, including those with his own family. These outcasts go into such an intense stress response that their circulatory systems collapse. They literally die from fear, often within just a few days.

Exploring the stress response further, another scientist, Hans Selye, found that in addition to the changes that take place in the nervous system, many important hormones jump into the fray. These hormones affect every aspect of the body, including the heart, stomach, liver, sex organs, and immune system. If the stress is long and drawn out, the entire physiology becomes exhausted, the body is unable to maintain balance, and something eventually breaks down.

Prolonged stress can make you sick and can accelerate aging. Over time, the stress response can cause high blood pressure, heart disease, stomach ulcers, autoimmune diseases, cancer, anxiety, insomnia, and depression. This may lead you to ask, if the fight-or-flight response is so damaging, why did nature create it? The original purpose of the fight-or-flight response was to help mankind survive in threatening situations. If a ferocious animal was about to eat you, the only way to survive was to either fight back or run away. Considering that human beings do not have thick hides, large canines, or big tusks, our ability to quickly react to a threat helped us survive in a dangerous environment.

Today, this response is still occasionally useful, as when a fireman goes into a burning building to rescue a child, or when you leap out of the way of a reckless driver speeding on a residential street. Most of the time, however, the fight-or-flight response no longer serves us very well. You may activate the stress response when you are stuck in rush-hour traffic or facing a critical work deadline, but neither fighting nor running away is a viable option. The pressure to do something without a way to release it causes harm. The long-term consequences of an activated stress response speed up the aging process and makes us susceptible to illness.

The opposite of the fight-or-flight response is the *restful response.* There are two kinds of restful responses: restful awareness and restful sleep. Restful awareness is the state when your body/mind system is in deep rest but your mind is awake. Restful sleep is the state in which your body/mind system is in deep rest and your mind is sleeping. Both of these states renew the body, although some studies indicate that restful awareness may provide even deeper rest than sleep. However, for our purpose of age reversal, both experiences are equally important. Restful awareness occurs during meditation. Restful sleep includes both dream sleep and dreamless deep sleep. Your subjective experience of the restful response is relaxation. The physiological changes that occur are:

- Your heart rate slows.
- Your blood pressure normalizes.
- You consume less oxygen.
- You use oxygen more efficiently.
- You expel less carbon dioxide.
- Your breathing slows.
- Your heart pumps less blood.
- You perspire less.
- Your adrenal glands produce less adrenaline and noradrenaline.
- Your adrenal glands produce less cortisol.
- You make more sex hormones, particularly dehydroepiandrosterone (DHEA).
- Your pituitary gland releases more growth hormone (an antiaging hormone).
- Your immune function improves.

The Restful Awareness Response

Restful awareness is a natural mind/body response, as natural as the stress responses. The most direct way to experience restful awareness is through meditation. Meditation has been a part of Eastern cultures for thousands of years, but it is comparatively new in the West. Despite its recent arrival here, many studies have shown that anyone can easily learn to meditate and enjoy the physiological changes of experienced meditators.

The bodily changes of restful awareness in meditation are almost the exact opposite of the fight-or-flight response. During meditation, breathing slows, blood pressure decreases, and stress hormone levels fall. The consumption of oxygen during meditation falls almost twice as much as during sleep. What is fascinating about these physiological changes is that even as the body is resting deeply in meditation, the mind is awake, though quiet. Brain wave studies show improved coherence between different parts of the brain during meditation. These changes in body and mind are not seen during wakefulness or sleeping. The unique combination of physical relaxation and an alert yet quiet mind explains the term *restful awareness* and distinguishes this state from restful sleep.

People who regularly experience restful awareness develop less hypertension, heart disease, anxiety, and depression. They find it easier to give up life-damaging habits such as cigarettes, excessive alcohol, and drugs. They also show improvements in their immune function and reduced susceptibility to infections. Research on people who meditate demonstrates wide-ranging health improvements and a reversal in many of the biomarkers of aging.

Studies have shown that the longer people have been practicing meditation, the younger they score on tests of biological age. For example, long-term meditators show biological ages almost twelve years younger than their chronological age. Other studies have shown that certain hormonal changes usually associated with aging can be slowed or reversed through regular meditation. One of the most interesting ones found that the hormone DHEA is higher in people who meditate than those who do not. We know that levels of DHEA steadily fall as we age. This has led some people to suggest that supplementing the diet with this hormone can reverse aging. We believe it is better to raise your DHEA levels through meditation than supplementation. There is good evidence that you can reverse your biological age by taking time to quiet your mind and experience the restful response.

It should be obvious that the restful awareness response (meditation) is a very important way to reverse the aging process. Although you may wonder when you'll ever find the time to meditate, we strongly encourage you to make meditation an important part of your life. It will actually create more time for you, because you will be much more efficient when your mind is calm and centered. We recommend twenty minutes of restful awareness (sitting meditation with your eyes closed) twice a day. The best times to meditate are shortly after awakening in the morning, and again in the later afternoon or early evening. The morning meditation starts your day with a fresh, calm mental attitude. The late afternoon or evening session helps freshen your mind after a day's activity.

The time you take to experience restful awareness will yield immediate rewards. You will notice relaxation during the meditation and increased energy and creativity during your day. If you have not meditated before, start with the So Hum meditation technique. After you have practiced this procedure for a while, we recommend you learn a more specific and personalized process called Primordial Sound Meditation (PSM), taught by one of our certified instructors. PSM uses individualized mantras that are based on the time, date, and place of your birth. There are now over five hundred certified Primordial Sound Meditation teachers in the world. See the appendix for information on finding a PSM teacher in your area.

So Hum Meditation

1. Sit comfortably, where you will not be disturbed, and close your eyes.
2. Take a slow deep breath through your nose while thinking the word *So.*
3. Exhale slowly through your nose while thinking the word *Hum*.
4. Continue breathing easily, silently repeating, "So . . . Hum . . ." with each inflow and outflow of your breath.
5. Whenever your attention drifts to thoughts in your mind, sounds in your environment, or sensations in your body, gently return to your breath, silently repeating "So . . . Hum."
6. Continue this process for twenty minutes with an attitude of effortlessness and simplicity.
7. When the time is up, continue to sit with your eyes closed for a few more minutes before resuming your daily activity.

When practicing this technique, you will have one of several experiences. Regardless of your experience, have an attitude of "no resistance." Relinquish your need to control or anticipate what is occurring during the practice. Any of the following experiences are indications that you are meditating correctly:

1. Your attention is on your breathing as you silently repeat the mantra "So Hum."
2. Your mind drifts off into a stream of thoughts. Sometimes these thoughts will be almost dreamlike and other times you may feel that you are just thinking with your eyes closed. In either case, when you remember that your attention has drifted away from your breath and the mantra, gently return to it.
3. Occasionally at first, and more regularly after a while, you will have the experience of a thoughtless state. Your mind is silent and your body is deeply relaxed. We call this "going into the gap," or the experience of timeless mind. With regular practice, the inner silence you experience in the gap will infuse every aspect of your life.
4. There may be times in your meditation when you fall asleep. Because meditation is a gentle, natural process, if your body is

fatigued, it will take this opportunity to sleep. Listen to this message from your body and commit to getting the deep rest you need.

One of the most common complaints of a new meditator is "I am having too many thoughts." Thoughts are a part of meditation and you cannot force your mind to stop thinking. Just let the thoughts come and go and before long you will find your mind quieting. When you first begin meditation, you will experience relaxation while sitting with your eyes closed, but may revert to your typical stressful reactions when resuming your usual activities. Over time, more of the restful awareness gained in meditation will carry over into your life. As you face the daily challenges of being human, you'll find it easier to maintain your calm center. As you learn to avoid unnecessary and overreactive stress responses, you'll slow the aging process.

The restful alertness response reverses the aging process.

Restful Sleep

In addition to restful awareness, you need a minimum of six to eight hours of restful sleep each night. Restful sleep means that you drift off easily once you turn off the light and sleep soundly through the night. If you have to get up to go to the bathroom during the night, you are able to easily get back to sleep. You will know you have had restful sleep if upon awakening you feel energetic, alert, and vibrant. If you feel tired and unenthusiastic when you wake up in the morning, you have not had a night of restful sleep.

Restful sleep provides the foundation for your mental and physical well-being. Millions of people suffer with some form of insomnia, resulting in fatigue, lack of mental alertness, and weakened physical and mental health. It also contributes to both minor and major injury accidents. Studies have shown that if you wake up at three in the morning and do not get back to sleep, your immune cells do not work as well for the next twenty-four hours. Once you have a full night of sound sleep, they regain their disease-fighting abilities. Like the rest of you, your immune cells get tired and need their rest.

It takes just a small shift in your attention and behavior to have sound, restful sleep each night. Not gaining restful sleep is usually a result of poor habits. By changing your habits, you will avoid the entropy that comes with fatigue and enliven the creativity, vitality, and age-reversing benefits that come with restful sleep.

Preparing for Restful Sleep

After a day of stimulating activity your body is ready for and needs deep sleep. Aim for a nightly six to eight hours of sound slumber without the aid of medication. Hours of sleep before midnight are generally the most rejuvenating. Therefore, if you are sleeping eight hours between ten P.M. and six A.M., you will feel more rested than if you slept eight hours between midnight and eight A.M. To promote restful sleep, try the following routine:

Evening Routine

- Eat a relatively light dinner. This should be no later than seven P.M. so you do not go to bed on a full stomach.
- Take a leisurely stroll after dinner.
- To the extent possible, minimize exciting, aggravating, or mentally intensive activities after 8:30 P.M.

Bedtime

- Aim to be in your bed with the lights out between 9:30 P.M. and 10:30 P.M. If you are not used to getting to bed this early, move your bedtime up by half an hour every week until you are in bed by 10:30 P.M. For example, if you usually watch television until midnight, try shutting it off by 11:30 for a week. Then aim for a half hour earlier, and finally 10:30 P.M.

- About an hour before bedtime, run a hot bath into which you place a few drops of a calming aromatherapy essential oil such as lavender, sandalwood, or vanilla. You can also diffuse this scent in your bedroom.
- As your bath is running, perform a slow self-administered oil massage, using sesame or almond oil (see the massage description on pages 74–76).
- After your massage, soak in the warm tub for ten to fifteen minutes.
- While soaking, have the lights low or burn a candle, and listen to soothing music (see our recommendations in the appendix).
- After your bath, drink something warm. It can be a cup of warm milk with nutmeg and honey, or some chamomile or valerian root tea. If you desire, have a small cookie or . . .
- If your mind is very active, journal for a few minutes before bed, "downloading" some of your thoughts and concerns so you don't need to ruminate about them when you shut your eyes.
- Read inspirational or spiritual literature for a few minutes before bed. Avoid dramatic novels or distressing reading material.
- Do not watch television or do any work in bed.
- Once in bed, close your eyes and simply "feel

your body"—this means focus on your body and wherever you notice tension, consciously relax that area.
- Then, simply watch your slow easy breathing until you fall asleep.

Contingency Plan

- If you still have trouble falling asleep, try putting something warm on your belly in the area of the solar plexus. Use a warm water bottle or heating pad to soothe your body and calm your mind.
- Try silently repeating the sleeping mantra: Om Agasthi Shahina (Ōm Ah-gah′-stee Shah-ee′-nah).
- Try sleeping on your stomach with your feet hanging over the edge of the bed. On cold nights, wear socks so your toes stay warm.
- If you wake up during the night and have trouble getting back to sleep, try reclining in a soft, comfortable chair with a blanket. You may find it easier to drift off in a slightly upright position.
- If all else fails and you continue to have disrupted sleep, try staying up all night and avoid napping the following day. By nine P.M. the next evening, your mind and body will be ready to sleep. This can often reset your biological rhythms.

It is helpful to remember that if you are lying still in bed, silently repeating the sleeping mantra, your metabolic activity is nearly as low as if you were in deep sleep. Even if your mind is still somewhat active, your body is getting the deep rest it needs. Therefore, do not worry if you are not immediately falling asleep; by not worrying, you will quickly drift off into a deep slumber.

Lack of restful sleep accelerates aging.
Restful sleep accelerates healing,
minimizes entropy, and enlivens renewal.

Performing a Self-Massage

A massage gives you access to your inner pharmacy. Your skin is a rich source of age-reversing hormones that can be released through massage. A slow, calming massage releases natural relaxing chemicals. A brisk, invigorating massage releases natural energizing chemicals. We recommend self-massage as a valuable age-reversing component of your daily routine. To help you sleep at at night, perform your massage with gentle, soothing strokes. To help you get going in the morning, perform your massage more vigorously. If you are trying to lose unwanted pounds, you can also do this massage using a loofah, a defoliating scrub mitt.

FULL MASSAGE

This entire massage requires just a few tablespoons of warm oil. Begin by massaging your scalp, using small circular strokes as if shampooing your hair. With gentle strokes apply the oil to your forehead, cheeks, and chin, and then move to your ears. Slowly massage the back of your ears and your temples—this has a soothing effect.

Massage a small amount of oil onto the front and back of your neck and then move to your shoulders. When massaging your arms, use circular motions at the shoulders and elbows, and long back-and-forth motions on the upper arms and forearms.

Using large, gentle circular motions, massage your chest, stomach, and abdomen. Use an up-and-down motion over your breastbone. Applying a bit of oil to both hands, gently reach around to massage your back and spine as best you can.

As with your arms, massage your legs with a circular motion at the ankles and knees, using a straight back-and-forth motion on the long parts. Use whatever oil remains to massage your feet, paying extra attention to your toes.

Mini-Massage

Your head and feet are the most important parts of your body to massage in preparation for restful sleep. Using a tablespoon of warm oil, gently rub it into your scalp, using the small, circular motions described above. Soothingly massage your forehead from side to side with your palm. Gently massage your temples, then the outside of your ears. Spend a little time massaging the back and front of your neck.

With a second tablespoon of oil, slowly but firmly massage the soles of your feet. Work the oil around your toes with your fingertips. Sit quietly for a few moments to soak in the oil, and then take your warm bath.

Harmonize Your Biological Rhythms with the Rhythms of Nature

Nature operates in seasons, cycles, and rhythms. Everything in this world moves through periods of activity and rest, including your physiology. Our planet has cycles of day and night, as well as seasonal cycles. When your biological rhythms are aligned with the rhythms of nature, your body/mind system feels invigorated and healthy. When your biorhythms are not aligned with natural cycles, you generate wear and tear in your body and mind, accelerating the aging process.

Technology that runs on electricity has been around for only a century, and yet many people's daily schedules revolve around late-night television shows, all-night markets, microwave ovens, and alarm clocks. Their daily routines are out of synch with nature. Just as jet lag results in mood changes, concentration problems, and digestive disturbances, an irregular daily routine affects your mind and body. Depression, insomnia, anxiety, constipation, bloating, and weakened immunity are the result.

You can align your biological rhythms with those of nature by paying attention to a few basic principles. These are:

Morning Routine

- Wake up without an alarm clock. The best way to do this is to leave your bedroom shades or curtains partially open so the morning sunlight arouses you.
- Empty your bladder and bowels first thing in the morning. Drinking a glass of warm water will help stimulate elimination.
- Perform your morning exercise routine (see Chapter 7).
- Take your shower preceded or followed by an oil massage.
- Meditate for twenty to thirty minutes.
- Eat your breakfast when you are hungry.

Midday Routine

- Eat your lunch consciously.
- Eat a bigger meal at noontime compared to your dinner.
- Take a ten-minute walk after lunch.

Early Evening Routine

- Meditate for twenty to thirty minutes before you eat your dinner, and then follow the evening routine described earlier in this chapter.

You can also benefit by aligning yourself with the seasonal cycles. As the days become shorter during the late fall and winter months, make some different choices to balance the changes in your environment.

Harmonizing your biological rhythms with the rhythms of nature minimizes entropy and reverses aging.

Winter Routine

- Get to bed earlier.
- Increase your intake of warmer foods—soups, casseroles, hot cereals—to balance the coldness of winter.
- Drink plenty of warm liquids—ginger and other herbal teas.
- Perform your daily oil massage, leaving a thin layer of oil on your skin to protect against dryness.
- Keep your head covered when you go outside to prevent chills.
- If you get frequent colds during the winter season, try using a Neti pot and Nasya oil to cleanse and protect your nasal passages (see description on following page).

Using a Neti Pot and Nasya

Using a Neti pot and Nasya is a traditional method to purify and revitalize the breathing passages. In the same way that massage nourishes and rejuvenates the skin, Neti and Nasya nourish and rejuvenate the breathing passages. This process can reduce allergies and decrease your chances of contracting upper-respiratory infections. It is also useful before traveling on a plane, to keep your breathing passages moist.

A Neti pot is a small container with a spout that can be gently placed into your nostrils through which warm salt water is administered. Usually made from a ceramic material, a typical Neti pot holds about $^{2}/_{3}$ of a cup of water to which $^{1}/_{8}$ of a teaspoon of salt is added.

Place the spout of the Neti pot in one nostril and gently pour in the warm salt water. Your head should be positioned so the water runs out the other nostril. Any remaining liquid in your nasal passages is expelled and the process is repeated on the other side.

continued

Nasya involves the application of a few drops of oil to the nasal membranes. The oil should be an edible grade of sesame, almond, or olive. Herbalized aromatic oils that contain small amounts of camphor, eucalyptus, and menthol can also be used. Place a drop of the oil on your pinkie finger and apply it inside your nostril. Then gently sniff it up and repeat on the other side. This can be repeated four to six times a day.

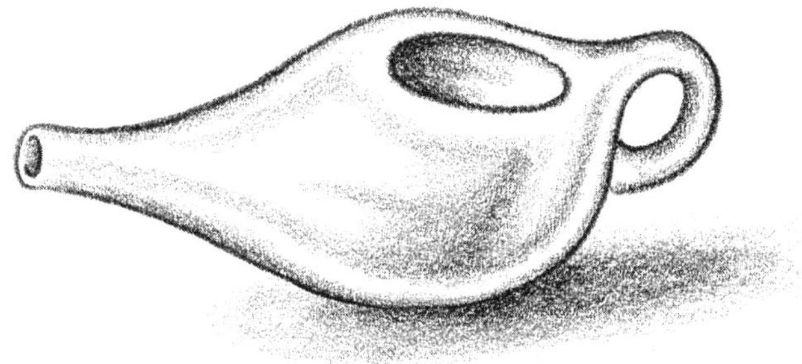

Neti Pot

During the warmer summer months, you can take other steps to maintain your balance while paying attention to the changing signals from your environment.

Summer Routine

- Drink plenty of fresh water throughout the day.
- Eat an abundant amount of locally grown fresh fruits and juices.
- Generally eat lighter.
- Perform your exercise early in the morning before it gets too hot.
- Spend more time outdoors, particularly in the evening when the day cools down.
- You can go to bed a little later, in alignment with longer daylight hours.

Dynamic activity during the day leads to restful sleep at night. Remember, you are not separate from Nature; you are a part of Nature. Tune in to the rhythms of nature and you will reverse your biological age.

Every day in every way,
I am increasing my mental and physical capacity.
My Biostat is set at a healthy ____ years of age.
I look and feel a healthy ____ years old.

I am reversing my biological age:

- *By changing my perception of my body, its aging and time; and*
- *Through two kinds of deep rest—restful awareness and restful sleep.*

4

You Can Reverse Your Biological Age by Lovingly Nurturing Your Body Through Healthy Food

ACTION STEP #3

I am reversing my biological age by lovingly nurturing my body through healthy food.

I put this into practice by:

1. *Enjoying the six tastes.*
2. *Eating consciously.*
3. *Honoring the signals of hunger and satiety in my body.*

Food can heal and renew.
Food can be your antiaging medicine.

Nurturing your body through healthy food is the third step to reverse the aging process. Next to breathing, eating is the most natural thing in the world, and yet many people are confused about their nutrition. Should you be eating more protein or more complex carbohydrates? Is dairy good or bad for you? Should you be eating your vegetables raw, or are they better for you cooked? Considering how much conflicting information is around, it is not surprising if you are perplexed about the best diet.

When it comes to aging, there is a steady flow of new nutritional programs promoting their advantages over others, but there is honestly little evidence to suggest that one approach is clearly more beneficial than another. We do know, based on reliable research, that if you eat an abundance of fresh vegetables, fruits, and whole grains, while reducing your intake of animal fat, you will increase your chances of living healthier and longer. The key to a diet that will reverse the aging process is to eat foods that are both very healthy and very delicious. A successful program must also be flexible, for any diet that is difficult to follow will not be practical and you will not stick with it for long. The nutritional program we present here has these essential components: it is nutritionally balanced, it is sumptuous, and it is easy to follow whether you are cooking for yourself or regularly eating at restaurants.

Your body is a field of energy, transformation, and intelligence made out of the food you eat. A sugar molecule in the apple you ate at lunch yesterday may be a part of your stomach lining today. An amino acid from the side order of cottage cheese you ate may now be in a fiber in your bicep muscle. An iron molecule from your spinach salad may already be part of the hemoglobin in one of your red blood cells. You become what you eat.

One of four things happens to every molecule you ingest: (1) it is transformed into a structural part of your body; (2) it is used for energy; (3) it is stored for possible future use; or (4) it is eliminated. If you are building a new house, you want the best lumber. If you are building a new body, you want the best food. Eating to reverse aging is not difficult. It just requires enough attention and intention to ensure that you are receiving the highest quality sources of energy and intelligence to create a healthy body.

You become what you eat.

Making Sense of Taste

We encourage you to follow a nutritional program that is expansive, not restrictive. We are aware of the many dietary plans that tell you to avoid certain types of food. The most common restriction diets we hear about at the Chopra Center include avoiding dairy, avoiding wheat, and avoiding all sugars. Other programs recommend the elimination of nightshade vegetables or any food that is acidic.

If you know for certain that you have problems with a specific food, listen to your body. If, however, you have eliminated certain foods only because you were told or read they were harmful, you may want to gently reintroduce them as part of a balanced diet and see for yourself if they are good or bad for you. Listening to your body is the best way to assess the suitability of any food.

According to Ayurveda, all foods can be categorized into one or more of six basic tastes. These six flavors are:

Sweet
Sour
Salty
Pungent
Bitter
Astringent

The first basic principle of an age-reversing diet is to ensure that throughout the day you consume foods from all six taste groups. These are the tastes that nature has created to provide the basic building blocks you need to nourish your body. The energy and intelligence of the natural world is packaged for your consumption in these six tastes. Let's look at each taste group in more detail.

Sweet

Foods that provide the sweet taste are rich in carbohydrates, proteins, and fats. Grains, cereals, breads, pastas, nuts, milk, dairy, fish, fowl, red meat, and oils are all classified as sweet foods. Sweet fruits include bananas, cherries, papayas, mangoes, peaches, pears, and raisins. Examples of sweet vegetables, which contain a predominance of complex carbohydrates, are artichokes, asparagus, carrots, cauliflower, okra, squash, and sweet potatoes. All food from animal sources is considered sweet. If you examine your grocery cart at the checkout counter, you'll recognize that you consume a greater volume of foods in this category of flavors than any other.

Since the sweet category covers a wide range of potentially edible substances from candy to quinoa, it is important to consume sweet foods that are balancing and nutritious. In general this means:

- Favor foods rich in complex carbohydrates, particularly whole grains, breads, cereals, rice, and pasta. Aim for eight helpings a day. A piece of rye toast, half a cup of pasta, one whole wheat tortilla, half a bagel, half a cup of rice, and a small potato are examples of one complex carbohydrate serving.
- Consume at least three to five servings of fresh fruit each day. One peach, one pear, one banana, half a cup of cherries, and half a cantaloupe are examples of one fruit serving.
- Consume at least five servings of vegetables each day. A half-cup of most cooked vegetables and a cup of most greens constitute one vegetable serving. Choose from a wide variety of green and yellow vegetables.
- Choose more vegetable sources of protein, including beans, legumes, seeds, and nuts. Although nuts are high in fat, most of it is

polyunsaturated or monosaturated, which is better for you. Nuts contain many beneficial phytochemicals and have been shown to lower cholesterol levels.

- Favor nonfat and low-fat milk and dairy products.
- If you eat meat, minimize your intake of red meat, substituting cold-water fishes and lean fowl.

There is considerable controversy these days regarding the ideal balance of carbohydrates, proteins, and fats. Advocates of very low-fat diets refer to studies showing that coronary heart disease can be reversed and cancer can be prevented by lowering the intake of saturated fat. Low-carbohydrate advocates suggest that there is an unprecedented abundance of sugars in the modern Western diet, resulting in abnormally high insulin levels, contributing to obesity and diabetes. Although there is validity to the basic premise of both extremes, we take the position that a balanced diet is the most healthful, most likely to result in sustained ideal body weight, and the only one that can be followed for a lifetime. With this in mind, our recommendation is to have a good mix of carbohydrates, proteins, and fats. Although the reversal of aging program does not require or encourage calorie counting, following our recommendations will result in a diet that is approximately 60 to 68 percent carbohydrates, 15 to 20 percent proteins, and 20 to 25 percent fats. (If you want to calculate your targeted intake of sweet food sources, see the box on page 94.)

Favor complex carbohydrates, vegetable and marine sources of protein, and vegetable and fish sources of fat and oils. Your cooking oils should be either monounsaturated, such as olive oil, or polyunsaturated, such as canola, safflower, or sunflower. A small amount of clarified butter (under one tablespoon per day) adds flavor with an acceptable dose of cholesterol. In addition to reducing your intake of saturated fats, this plan naturally increases your consumption of fiber-rich foods, which are helpful in normalizing elimination, lowering cholesterol levels, and reducing the risk of digestive tract cancers.

There are foods that accelerate
aging and entropy,
and others that renew and
revitalize the body.

Eating to Grow Younger

Use a calculator to compute your targets.

Calculate your daily calories by multiplying your weight in pounds by 16.

__________ × 16 = __________

Weight in pounds — Daily caloric needs

Calculate your carbohydrate intake by multiplying your daily calories by 0.16.

__________ × 16 = __________

Daily caloric needs — Grams of carbohydrates

Calculate your protein intake by multiplying your daily calories by 0.041.

__________ × 0.041 = __________

Daily caloric needs — Grams of carbohydrates

Calculate your fat intake by multiplying your daily calories by 0.023.

__________ × 0.023 = __________

Daily caloric needs — Grams of fat

Example: If you weigh 150 pounds, your numbers would look as follows:

1. Basic caloric needs:
   150 pounds × 16 = 2400 calories
2. Daily carbohydrate intake:
   2400 × 0.16 = 384 grams
3. Daily protein intake:
   2400 × 0.041 = 98 grams
4. Maximum fat intake:
   2400 × 0.023 = 55 grams

This plan results in the following calorie breakdown:

CALORIE SOURCE	GRAMS	CALORIES	% DAILY CALORIES
Carbohydrates	384	1536	64
Proteins	98	392	16
Fat	55	495	20

Sour

The sour taste results from the chemical action of organic acids on the taste buds. All acids are perceived as sour including citric acid, ascorbic acid (vitamin C), and acetic acid (vinegar). A regular dose of sour awakens your appetite and enhances your digestion. It also slows the emptying of your stomach, reducing the insulin-stimulating effect of carbohydrates. Although foods ranging from cheddar cheese to vinegar carry the sour taste, the best sources are fresh fruits including apples, apricots, berries, cherries, grapefruit, grapes, lemons, oranges, pineapples, and tomatoes. Low- and nonfat yogurt is also a good source of the sour taste. Fresh yogurt provides acidophilus bacteria, which are helpful in balancing your digestive tract.

Sour foods are usually excellent sources of vitamin C and flavonoids, which protect against heart disease and cancer. They also provide soluble fiber, which may reduce the chances of both coronary heart disease and diabetes. Many fermented condiments, such as pickles, green olives, and chutneys also carry the sour taste. Although they are helpful in stimulating digestion, they are best taken in small amounts. Get the bulk of your servings of sour through abundant helpings of tart fruits with less from salad dressings and pickled and fermented foods.

SALTY

Mineral salts are an essential component of health, but a typical Western diet is much more likely to have too much rather than too little salt. The salty taste promotes digestion, is mildly laxative, and has a mildly relaxing effect. Too much salt is associated with an increased risk for high blood pressure and may play a minor role in the development of osteoporosis.

In addition to common table salt, the salty taste is carried in fish, soy sauce, tamari, seaweed products, and most sauces. Be aware of your salt intake, recognizing that it is an essential taste but one that must be taken in moderation.

PUNGENT

The pungent or spicy taste is usually referred to as "hot." Most cultures recognize the value of the spicy taste, although Americans tend to be shy about it. The pungent spices have always been sought and valued. One of the major motivations for the journey of Christopher Columbus was to discover a shortcut to the exotic spices of India, which were prized by western Europeans.

The spicy flavor usually results from essential oils that are rich in antioxidant properties. Their ability to neutralize decay-causing free radicals may explain why pungent spices were commonly used to preserve food. The natural chemicals in hot spices are also antibacterial.

Modern scientific research has shown that natural compounds contained within spicy food sources such as onions, leeks, chives, and garlic may help lower your cholesterol level and blood pressure. Other studies have found that these pungent foods can protect you from cancer-causing agents in the environment. Chilis, ginger, horseradish, mustard, black and red pepper, radishes, and many culinary spices including basil, cinnamon, cloves, cumin, oregano, peppermint, rosemary, and thyme all carry the pungent taste. Use them liberally in your diet for both their flavor and the age-reversing benefits they bring to your health.

Bitter

Green and yellow vegetables are the primary source of the bitter taste. Common examples include bell peppers, broccoli, celery, chard, eggplant, endive, spinach, and zucchini. Most green leafy vegetables range from mildly to very bitter. Bitterness reflects the many natural chemicals contained in vegetables that have a wide range of age-reversing and health-enhancing effects. These phytochemicals (*phyto* is Greek for plant) help detoxify carcinogens, lower serum cholesterol levels, and enhance your immunity.

All vegetables carry essential vitamins and minerals. Green vegetables are good sources of B vitamins and folate, now known to play an important role in protecting against heart disease. Vegetables are an important source of both soluble and insoluble fiber. The soluble fiber is good for your heart and the insoluble fiber improves the movement of food through your digestive tract. High-fiber diets are associated with a lower risk for breast and digestive tract cancers.

The American Cancer Society recommends a minimum of five helpings of fruits and vegetable each day, but some studies have shown that less than 10 percent of Americans regularly follow this advice. We echo what mothers have been saying since the dawn of humanity: eat your vegetables.

Many herbs also carry the bitter taste and are important components of a healthy, balanced diet. Chamomile, cilantro, coriander, cumin, dill, fenugreek, licorice, rhubarb, rosemary, saffron, sage, tarragon, and turmeric are examples of culinary herbs and spices that contain the bitter flavor. Most medicinal herbs such as echinacea, aloe, black cohosh, gentian, goldenseal, licorice, passionflower, skullcap, and Saint-John's-wort are predominantly bitter due to their high concentrations of phytochemicals. Most people are not naturally attracted to the bitter taste, but small quantities enhance the taste of food and contribute to your well-being.

On the following page is a chart that highlights

a few of the amazing health-enhancing, age-reversing chemicals that fruits and vegetables provide.

PHYTOCHEMICAL	ACTIONS	SOURCES
Flavonoids	Antioxidant, anti-carcinogenic, protect against heart disease	Onions, broccoli, red grapes, apples, cherries, citrus fruits, berries, tomatoes
Phenolic compounds	Antioxidant, inhibit cancerous changes	Nuts, berries, green tea
Sulfides	Anticarcinogenic, inhibit blood clotting	Garlic, onions, chives
Lycopene	Anticarcinogenic	Tomatoes, red grapefruit
Isothiocyanates	Inhibit cancer growth	Broccoli, cabbage, cauliflower
Isoflavones	Block hormonally stimulated cancers, lower cholesterol levels.	Soybeans and soy-derived foods
Anthocyanins	Antioxidant, lower cholesterol, stimulate immunity	Berries, cherries, grapes, currants
Terpenoids	Antioxidant, antibacterial, prevent stomach ulcers	Peppers, cinnamon, horseradish, rosemary, thyme, turmeric

ASTRINGENT

Astringent foods produce a puckering effect on our mucous membranes. Although modern science does not classify the astringent property as an actual taste, the natural chemicals that produce astringency have many health-enhancing effects. Examples of foods that carry the astringent taste include apples, artichokes, asparagus, beans, bell peppers, buttermilk, celery, cherries, cranberries, cucumbers, figs, lemons, lentils, mung beans, mushrooms, pomegranates, potatoes, soybeans, spinach, green and black tea, tofu, whole wheat and rye grain products. Foods with the astringent taste have a compacting effect on your physiology and are important in the regulation of digestive function and wound healing.

Recent studies have found that the phytochemicals contained in both green and black tea, good sources of the astringent taste, may help protect you against a variety of illnesses, from cancer to heart disease. Beans, legumes, and peas are excellent sources of complex carbohydrates. They provide good-quality vegetable protein along with both soluble and insoluble fiber. Beans and legumes also supply us with folic acid, calcium, and magnesium.

One of the major shifts in diet between the

beginning of the twentieth and twenty-first centuries was a reduction in vegetable sources of protein and replacement by animal ones. With this change has come an increased risk for both heart disease and cancer. Add one or two servings of beans, peas, or lentils to your diet each day and you will grow younger and live longer.

Summary of the Six Tastes

TASTE	SOURCE
Sweet	*Favor:* whole grains, breads, fruits, starchy vegetables, low-fat organic dairy *Reduce:* refined sugars, animal fat
Sour	*Favor:* citrus fruits, berries, tomatoes *Reduce:* pickled and fermented foods, alcohol
Salty	*Reduce:* highly salted foods like potato chips, pretzels, processed tomato juice
Pungent	*Favor:* all spicy foods in small amounts—ginger, peppers, onions, peppermint, cinnamon
Bitter	*Favor:* all green and yellow vegetables
Astringent	*Favor:* beans, peas, lentils, apples, berries, figs, green tea *Reduce:* excessive coffee

The body is satisfied when it has access to the six tastes of life.

Delicious and Nutritious

It is easy to follow a dietary plan that conforms to the six tastes program. Regardless of the type of food you enjoy eating, you can both enhance its sumptuousness and health-promoting qualities by ensuring that your meals have a wide variety of tastes. Here are examples of meals representing a wide range of ethnic cuisine to demonstrate the practicality of this approach.

Seven Vegetarian Meals Representing the World's Regional Cuisines

See the full recipes at the end of the book.

Thai Cuisine

Clear Broth Soup with Coconut, Tofu, and Greens
Yellow Thai Curry with Carrots and Greens
Fresh Cucumber with Basil and Mint
Basmati Rice with Mangoes
Banana Coconut Stew

Chinese

Vegetable Hot and Sour Soup
Buddha's Feast

Marinated Sesame Tofu Strips
Simple Steamed Rice
Almond Cookies

Italian

White Bean and Vegetable Soup
Spinach and Eggplant Layered Pasta with Pesto
Garbanzo and Green Bean Stew
Roasted Carrots with Fresh Rosemary
Raspberry Tofu Sorbet

Mexican

Tortilla Soup with Avocado and Cilantro
Black Bean and Sweet Potato Enchiladas
Spanish Rice
Mango and Tomato Salsa
Baked Vanilla Flan with Maple Syrup

French

Creamy Asparagus Soup
Spinach, Leek, and Potato Tart
Braised Green Beans Amandine
Swiss Chard and Arugula with Lemon Tarragon Dressing
Poached Pears with Blackberries

American Bistro

Carrot Coriander Soup
Roasted Vegetable Barley Risotto
Cranberry and Sweet Potato Chutney
Organic Field Greens with Apple Vinaigrette
Cocoa Tofu Mousse with Almond Praline

Middle Eastern

Spinach and Lentil Soup
Hummus
Quinoa Tabouli
Creamy Tofu Cucumber and Mint Raita
Ratatouille Stew
Maple Walnut Filo Triangles

Optimizing Digestion

We build our bodies from the food we eat, so it is important that we receive the full range of nutrients required to sustain our best health. According to Ayurveda, it is equally important that we have ideal *digestive power* if we are to make the best use of the food we ingest. The Sanskrit word for digestive power is *Agni.* The English word *ignite* is derived from Agni. Agni can be thought of as the transformational principle of the body. To ensure optimal digestion, we recommend you pay attention to a few simple principles that apply to how we eat. We call these the Eating Awareness Techniques (EATs).

Eating Awareness Techniques

Listen to Your Appetite

Your body sends messages to your mind to meet its needs. One of the most important signals the body sends is that of hunger. Although many people who have struggled to keep excessive pounds off view their appetite as an adversary, listening to and honoring its message is one of the most important aspects of a healthy nutritional plan. The rule is simple: Eat when you are hungry and stop when you are satisfied. If you think of your appetite as a gauge ranging from empty (0) to full (10), our recommendation is to eat when you are really hungry (at a level 2 to 3) and stop when you are comfortably full but *not* stuffed (6 to 7). By not filling your stomach to capacity, you allow your digestive power to work at an optimal level. Just as your clothes do not get fully clean if you overstuff your washing machine, your food will not be fully digested if you overstuff your stomach.

Many people eat because it is time to eat, not

because their bodies are asking for food. You wouldn't fill up your gas tank if it was still half full, yet many people eat even when they are still full from the previous meal. Start listening to your body. Its wisdom mirrors the wisdom of the cosmos.

Pay Attention

It is easy to overeat if your environment distracts you while you are eating. Although many of us were conditioned to eat while watching television, it is easy to lose awareness of your body and overeat when an engaging drama or exciting adventure story captures your attention. Similarly, eating while working on an intense project or business transaction will often result in missing the signals that your body has had enough food. Have the intention to protect your mealtimes so you can enjoy your food in a relaxing environment. If you suffer with digestive imbalances such as heartburn or irritable bowel syndrome, creating a calm, comfortable mealtime will improve your digestion.

Favor Fresh Foods

There are foods that accelerate aging and entropy and others that renew and revitalize the body. Generally, "dead" foods contribute to degeneration and decay, while fresh foods enhance regeneration and vitality. For most foods, the less time between harvesting and consumption, the more energy and intelligence it provides. This means minimizing canned, frozen, and packaged foods to whatever extent possible. We also discourage eating leftovers or microwaved meals.

Use Food to Feed Your Body, Not Your Emotions

From the day we are born, we associate food with safety and comfort. The breast or bottle offered us when we were uncomfortable soothed both our physical and emotional distress. It is natural then that, as adults, we resort to food when we are feeling stressed or anxious. Unfortunately, if you are trying to fill your need for love with food, you are unlikely to be very successful, and the unnecessary calories will be stored as fat. Use food to satisfy the energy needs of your body and develop nourishing relationships to satisfy the needs of your emotional heart. Both will thank you for being aware of the difference.

Eat More at Lunch, Less at Dinner

Your digestive power is strongest at noontime. You secrete stomach acid, bile salts, and pancreatic enzymes in cycles throughout the day that support the absorption and metabolism of essential nutrients from the food you consume. Until the industrial revolution, most people ate their main meal in the middle of the day with a lighter meal in the evening. Respecting this time-honored pattern can improve digestive function and enhance sleep. Try eating a larger lunch and a smaller dinner and see if you notice an improvement in your vitality and well-being.

Kindle and Balance Your Digestive Fire

Ayurveda compares your digestive processes to a fire in a fireplace. To have the best possible heat and light, the fire needs to be kindled and stoked. The same can be said for your digestive fire. We recommend kindling your digestive fire before each meal with an herbal aperitif. This simple recipe helps awaken the first stage of digestion, ensuring a good start to metabolizing your food. Try taking a shot glass full prior to each meal and you will notice a healthy boost to your digestive function.

Herbal Aperitif

Mix equal parts of lemon juice, ginger-root juice, water, and honey.

Add a pinch of black pepper.

Take a two-ounce shot of this herbal elixir right before your meal.

After each meal, we recommend a spice blend to help balance your digestive fire. This is easily prepared by mixing equal parts of roasted fennel seeds, cardamom seeds, cumin seeds, and a pinch of maple sugar. Chew on one-half teaspoon of this spice blend at the end of each meal to enhance your digestion.

In addition to the herbal aperitif before and the spice blend after each meal, try sipping on gingerroot tea throughout the day. Grate one-half teaspoon of fresh gingerroot per pint of hot water and try to consume two to three pints per day. Ginger has a general toning effect on the alimentary tract, enhancing digestion, absorption, and elimination. Ginger is known in Ayurveda as the universal medicine. If you have a tendency toward heartburn or indigestion, use ginger cautiously at first to ensure that your symptoms do not worsen.

How you eat is as important as what you eat.

Keep It Simple

Don't make nutrition complicated. It is not difficult to eat in a way that is nourishing and delicious. We can reduce this entire chapter into five simple principles:

1. Eat when you are hungry; stop when you are satiated.
2. Chew your food until it is liquid or semi-liquid before swallowing.
3. Don't put the next bite of food into your mouth until you've swallowed the previous one.
4. Don't put the next meal in your stomach until you've digested the previous one (usually at least three hours).
5. Eat food with all six tastes during the day.

Eating as Celebration

It is easy to become confused when considering the best diet to help you live a long and healthy life. There is a tremendous amount of conflicting information on nutrition with experts advocating a wide variety of approaches. Although every dietary program offers some nuggets of wisdom, for any approach to be truly successful, it has to be sustainable, delicious, balanced, and practical. Try following our nutritional recommendations for a month and observe the infusion of vitality into your body and mind. This program will help you grow younger and live longer.

Every day in every way,
I am increasing my mental and physical capacity.
My Biostat is set at a healthy ____ years of age.
I look and feel a healthy ____ years old.

I am reversing my biological age:

- *By changing my perception of my body, its aging and time;*
- *Through two kinds of deep rest—restful awareness and restful sleep; and*
- *By nurturing my body through healthy foods.*

5

You Can Reverse Your Biological Age by Using Nutritional Complements Wisely

ACTION STEP #4

I am reversing my biological age by taking nutritional complements that have a direct effect on the prevention of illness.

I put this into practice by:

1. *Learning about the biological effects of intelligent nutrients.*
2. *Ingesting the nutrients on a daily basis.*
3. *Performing daily rituals that focus my attention and intention to enhance the effects of the nutrients.*

Nutritional complements, wisely used
can prevent many age-related illnesses
and dramatically reverse
your biological age.

Although we'd like to believe that eating healthy foods is all you need in order to thrive, there is increasing evidence that the appropriate use of nutritional supplements may take you to a higher level of well-being than is achievable by food alone. Eating healthy is still more important than taking concentrated nutrients, which is why we like to call them *complements* rather than *supplements.* We use the term to remind you that these nutritional allies are not substitutes for good food; they take nutrition to a higher level. Because we now know that high levels of certain nutrients can lower your risk for many common health concerns associated with aging, nutritional complements play an important health-promoting role.

Your body is a field of energy, transformation, and intelligence. It is amazingly adept at acquiring, transforming, storing, and releasing energy. The primary sources of this energy are the carbohydrates, proteins, and fats contained in food. Food also provides natural chemicals—vitamins, minerals, and trace elements—that we require to use the energy available in food efficiently. Other nutritional components, such as antioxidant chemicals, are essential for protecting the cells and tissues from harmful inner or outer environmental toxins. Finally, as we discussed last chapter, many plant-based food sources contain phytochemicals, essential plant-derived substances that help protect us from a wide variety of illnesses.

People who receive adequate "doses" of essential nutrients through the food they eat generally live healthier, longer lives than those whose diet is nutritionally lacking. It is, however, becoming increasingly clear that some nutrients have additional benefits when available in quantities higher than those usually provided through diet. We have come to believe that complementing a well-balanced diet with supplemental nutrients can offer the best opportunity for maintaining and enhancing youthful vitality. Let's review the basics of nutritional supplementation.

Vitamins—The Vital Nutrients

Vitamins are organic substances required in tiny amounts to maintain health. Since they cannot be manufactured in the body, they must be ingested from outside sources. Government-sponsored nutritional panels have developed guidelines for thirteen vitamins and fifteen minerals. Many of the Recommended Daily Allowances (RDAs) are based upon levels that prevent a known vitamin-deficiency disease, even though several essential nutrients have health-promoting effects at levels considerably higher than currently recommended. Although there is a constant stream of new data on the appropriate role for nutritional supplements, we feel there is enough reliable information to offer practical, balanced suggestions. Our "bottom line" recommendations for nutritional supplementation are provided at the end of this chapter.

Water-Soluble Vitamins

Water-soluble vitamins include the B vitamins and vitamin C. They are stored in only limited amounts in bodily tissues, and therefore they need to be consumed on a daily basis. The B vitamins work with enzyme systems to metabolize food and form essential biochemicals. Each of the water-soluble vitamins, its important purpose, the symptoms and signs of its deficiency, food sources, and the RDA is listed in the table on pages 118-119.

VITAMIN	PURPOSE	DEFICIENCY SYMPTOMS AND SIGNS	FOOD SOURCES	RDA
B1 (Thiamin)	Metabolism of protein, carbohydrates, and fats	Fatigue, weight loss, weakness, heart problems, confusion, nerve problems	Whole wheat, nuts, beans, cauliflower, meats	1.0 to 1.5 mg
B2 (Riboflavin)	Fatty acid and amino acid metabolism	Mucous membrane irritation, eye changes, nerve problems	Dairy, eggs, green leafy vegetables, asparagus, fish, liver	1.2 to 1.8 mg
Niacin	Metabolism of carbohydrates, protein, and fats	Skin changes, diarrhea, nervous system problems	Milk, eggs, legumes, whole grains, poultry, meats	15 to 20 mg
B6 (Pyridoxine)	Amino acid and neurotransmitter metabolism	Weakness, nervous system problems, white blood cell problems	Soybeans, nuts, bananas, avocados, eggs, meats	1.4 to 2.2 mg
Folic acid	Amino acid metabolism, DNA synthesis	Anemia, weakness, mental changes, digestive disturbances	Dark green vegetables, peas, wheat germ, lima beans	400 mcg

B12 (Cobalamin)	Amino acid and fatty acid metabolism	Anemia, fatigue, nervous system problems	Milk, seafood, fermented soybeans, cheese, meats	2.0 mcg
Biotin	Protein, fat, and carbohydrate metabolism	Skin problems, heart problems, fatigue, anemia	Dairy, molasses, nuts	30 to 100 mcg
Pantothenic acid	Metabolism of fatty acids, neurotransmitters	Fatigue, digestive disturbances, nerve problems	Whole grains, cheese, beans, nuts, dates, fish, meats	4 to 7 mg
C (Ascorbic acid)	Antioxidant, formation of collagen, neuro-transmitter metabolism	Poor wound healing, bleeding, anemia	Citrus fruits, tomatoes, green leafy vegetables, peas	60 mg

Fat-Soluble Vitamins

The fat-soluble vitamins include A, D, E, K, and beta-carotene. They are stored in the liver and, as they are excreted slowly from the body, can accumulate to toxic levels. In appropriate doses the various fat-soluble vitamins are essential for maintaining immunity, bone strength, and blood clotting. The functions, deficiency consequences, common sources, and RDAs are listed on page 121.

Nutrients as Medicines

Nobody dies of old age; we die of the illnesses that are common in our older years. Although modern medicine is continually developing new approaches to treat the diseases that create suffering and shorten life, there is increasing evidence that nutritional approaches can help reduce our risk and lessen the disability caused by the common afflictions of humanity. In this section we will explore five prevalent conditions in which nutritional approaches may be helpful: heart disease, cancer, memory loss, arthritis, and immune weakness.

VITAMIN	PURPOSE	DEFICIENCY SYMPTOMS AND SIGNS	FOOD SOURCES	RDA
A	Maintains visual function, skin and mucous membrane integrity, enhances immunity	Skin problems, night blindness, weak bone formation	Dairy, yellow and green vegetables (carrots, squash, peppers) and orange fruits (apricots, papayas), egg yolks	4,000 to 5,000 IU
Carotenoids (Beta-carotene)	Antioxidants, enhance immunity	Increased risks for heart disease and cancer	Yellow and green vegetables (sweet potatoes, pumpkins) and orange fruits (cantaloupe, peaches)	Converted into vitamin A as needed
D (Chole-, ergo- calciferol)	Regulates calcium and phosphorus	Bone weakness	Fish oils, oily fish, fortified dairy, egg yolk, butter	200 to 400 IU
E (Alpha-, beta-, gamma- tocopherol)	Antioxidant, protects cell membranes	Nervous system, blood cell, and reproductive system problems	Vegetable and seed oils, whole grains, green leafy vegetables, wheat germ, egg yolks, butter, nuts	12 to 18 IU
K (Phyllo, mena- quinones	Helps synthesize blood-clotting factors	Prolonged clotting time, bleeding	Dark green leafy vegetables, broccoli, legumes	45 to 80 mcg

Nourishing Your Heart

Heart disease is the number-one cause of death and serious illness in our society. By now you must be aware that smoking, high blood pressure, an elevated serum cholesterol level, and lack of physical exercise all contribute to the risk for cardiovascular illness. Mental attitude in the form of hostility also plays a role in increasing your susceptibility to heart blockages. We'll address other lifestyle issues throughout this book, but let's focus here on the role of nutritional complements.

Antioxidant Vitamins and Heart Disease

Studies have shown that oxidized forms of cholesterol are more likely to be deposited into blood vessels, eventually resulting in blockage. Antioxidant vitamins can reduce the formation of "bad" cholesterol and may lower the risk of heart attacks. The roles of the three major antioxidant vitamins have been studied, with vitamin E showing the most benefit, vitamin C showing little benefit, and the carotenoids falling somewhere in between.

Studies on vitamin E over the past thirty years have generally confirmed its benefit in lowering the risk of heart attacks in daily doses ranging from 100 to 800 IU. In one of the largest studies, men taking 400 or 800 IU of vitamin E for an average of one and a half years showed a 47 percent reduction in heart attacks in both dosing groups. Most other studies involving both men and women have supported the benefits of vitamin E in reducing heart disease.

Although studies have suggested that diets naturally rich in beta-carotene provide some protection against heart disease, no study to date has convincingly shown that carotenoid supplementation provides definite benefit. In fact, in one large trial, smokers given beta-carotene and vitamin A supplementation actually showed an increase in lung cancer deaths and a slight increase in deaths from heart attacks. Although there continues to be a lot of debate about the meaning of this report, the bottom line regarding the carotenoids and heart disease is to eat your carrots, and not overdo supplementation.

Although vitamin C is clearly important in maintaining healthy blood vessels, studies have not consistently shown a benefit for supplemental C in reducing the risk of heart disease. As with the carotenoids, people following diets rich in natural sources of vitamin C have less heart disease than those whose diets are less abundant in fresh fruits and vegetables. We can guess that people whose diets are naturally plentiful in vitamin C may also be following generally healthy lifestyles, which cannot be replaced by vitamin supplementation alone.

A naturally occurring antioxidant that has been receiving increasing attention is coenzyme Q10 or CoQ10. It is also known as ubiquione, reflecting its *ubiquitous* presence in living systems. Studies have shown that it enhances the function of heart muscles and may be helpful for people with coronary artery disease, high blood pressure, and congestive heart failure. Although we do not yet know enough about this substance to recommend it for universal use, we do believe it is worth discussing with your health care adviser if you are facing heart disease.

Folate, B12, B6, Homocysteine, and Heart Disease

One of the most important recent nutritional discoveries is the recognition that an elevated blood level of the amino acid homocysteine is associated with a greater risk for heart disease. This amino acid may increase the development of atherosclerosis and the likelihood of blood clotting. The vitamins folic acid, B6, and B12 are important in reducing the circulating amount of homocysteine in the blood. Supplementation with folic acid (400 mcg to 5 mg) along with B6 and B12 can lower homocysteine levels and slow the development of coronary heart disease.

Keeping Away Cancer

Despite modern advances in the understanding, diagnosis, and treatment of cancer, this dreaded illness remains the second leading cause of death in our society. There are few more critical situations in life in which prevention can reap such great rewards. Although there is much about cancer we do not know, there is good information that diets rich in antioxidant nutrients have a protective effect against the inner and outer toxins that can trigger malignant cellular transformations. It is less clear that nutritional supplementation provides additional benefit. The following is our current position on the role of nutrients in cancer.

Vitamin A, Carotenoids, and Cancer

Although one might expect that people at high risk for cancer given beta-carotene would fare better, three different studies thus far have not been able to show a benefit. In both men and women smokers and in men exposed to asbestos, beta-carotene provided no protection against lung cancer, and two studies actually showed a higher risk among people taking carotenoids.

Laboratory studies have shown that vitamin A and various carotenoids may slow the growth of prostate, cervical, oral, and skin cancers, but studies documenting the clinical benefits of supplementation have not been convincing. One of the more interesting carotenoids is lycopene, found in highest concentrations in tomatoes. This potent antioxidant seems to confer protection against prostate cancer, providing a good incentive to get your helping of tomatoes on a regular basis. Our bottom line is to eat a diet that is naturally rich in carotenoids, using supplements judiciously to ensure a healthy baseline intake.

Vitamin E and Cancer

For many years, laboratory studies of animals have shown that vitamin E can reduce the incidence of various cancers, and have suggested it may be of benefit to people as well. A large study from China found that people taking daily supplemental doses of beta-carotene, vitamin E, and selenium had significantly lower rates of cancer compared to those on other nutritional regimens. Other reports have supported the view that vitamin E may protect against oral, throat, and prostate cancer. Getting a good daily helping of this powerful antioxidant is essential to maintain youthful well-being.

Vitamin C and Cancer

As is true with the other antioxidant vitamins, the evidence for vitamin C as a protector against cancer is greater in laboratory investigations than it is in clinical studies. There are suggestions that vitamin C can lower the risk of cancers of the female reproductive system, throat, digestive tract, and respiratory system, but whether these lab findings are relevant to people remains to be proven. Because it is generally well tolerated, even in exceptionally high doses, many nutritionists are advocating a higher recommended daily allowance than the 60 milligrams currently suggested.

Nutrients and Memory

We all consider clear thinking and a good memory essential for health and well-being. Good nutrition is an important aspect of mental clarity and a few nutritional supplements have been shown to be of benefit. Studies on vitamin E in both animals and humans have suggested that its antioxidant properties protect brain cells from toxic memory-damaging forces. A large study of older people showed a correlation between low vitamin E levels and problems with memory. People with Alzheimer's disease given vitamin E experience less deterioration. We are by and large convinced that getting your daily helping of vitamin E can help maintain mental sharpness.

The herb ginkgo biloba has been receiving increasing attention as a memory-enhancing agent. Derived from the oldest tree on earth, ginkgo can enhance mental performance in people with and without memory concerns. A standardized extract is now widely available and can be a helpful ally in keeping you on top of your mental game. The usual daily dose of ginkgo is between 120 and 240 milligrams per day. Because of rare reports of bleeding complications, ginkgo should not be mixed with blood thinning medications.

The brain chemical acetylcholine seems to play a particularly important role in memory, as it is involved in the storage, recall, and communication of information. For many years, scientists have attempted to enhance the function of acetylcholine using both synthetic and natural substances with modest results. The use of a soy-derived compound called phosphatidylserine (PS) may enhance the production of acetylcholine and has been shown to have a mild memory-enhancing effect. All commercially available phosphatidylserine is derived from soy. Studies showing a benefit for PS in enhancing memory have used about 300 milligrams per day. This substance is now available from a number of nutritional supplement companies.

Another nutritional supplement that may increase your levels of acetylcholine is acetyl-L-carnitine (ALC). This natural substance is important for the production of energy in muscle cells and seems to play a special role in brain cells. ALC has been researched in patients with Alzheimer's disease and was found to slow the progression of memory loss, particularly in younger patients. It has also been shown to improve memory decline in elderly subjects without definite dementia. In addition to helping with attention and certain learning skills, ALC has been reported helpful in reducing symptoms of depression.

In addition to the influence of carnitine on the mind and emotions, studies have suggested that it may enhance heart and nerve function in people with diabetes. Both L-carnitine and acetyl-L-carnitine are now available from a number of nutritional supplement companies, usually in the form of capsules containing 250 milligrams. Very few side effects other than digestive upset have been attributed to these substances. Studies on ALC in patients with Alzheimer's disease have used doses of 1 to 3 grams per day, and it may take months before any benefits are recognized. If you or a loved one are experiencing progressive memory loss, ALC may be worth a try, but otherwise, we do not believe you should routinely supplement your diet with an extra helping of carnitine.

Healthy Joint Nutrition

The vitality of youth implies the ability to move without discomfort. Joint pain and arthritis can interfere with your quality of life and make you feel older than you are. There is increasing information that nutritional approaches can enhance joint health and reduce the discomfort and disability of joint inflammation and degeneration. Vitamins A, C, D, and E all play important roles in protecting our joints from the wear and tear of movement. A recent study from the Arthritis Center at Boston University found that a higher intake of vitamin C, and to a lesser extent vitamin E and beta-carotene, was associated with less degenerative arthritis and pain. Other reports have suggested that the antioxidant properties of vitamin E can help to calm the inflammation of rheumatoid arthritis. The B vitamin niacinamide may also help to dampen the production of inflammatory chemicals shown to contribute to joint problems.

Fatty Acids and the Chemistry of Inflammation

Your blood is a rich soup of biochemicals, affected by the nutrients you consume. Chemicals known as cytokines are important in the regulation of inflammation and can be influenced by the types of fats and oils you ingest. Although the process is a complex one, there is increasing evidence that consuming more foods with omega-3 fatty acids may lower the level of undesired inflammatory reactions. Foods naturally rich in omega-3 fatty acids include flaxseed and cold-water fish such as salmon, albacore tuna, and herring. These foods also confer some protection against coronary heart disease.

The Joint Nutrients

Glucosamine sulfate is a natural constituent of cartilage. A number of studies looking into supplementing the diet with this substance have shown it can reduce pain and improve joint function. It is surprisingly well absorbed from the digestive tract and in many studies is as effective as standard anti-inflammatory medicines with fewer negative side effects. The usual dose of glucosamine sulfate is 500 milligrams three times daily.

The Nutrients of Immunity

Healthy immunity is both necessary for and reflective of our health and vitality. When the immune system is functioning at an optimal level, it responds to challenges proportionate to the threat, neither under- nor overreacting. Many reports have documented that aging is associated with altered immune function, which makes people susceptible to infections and cancer. In many ways, our ability to discriminate between potentially nourishing and toxic influences is the essence of a healthy immune system and a healthy life. To grow younger and live longer, it is essential that we maintain a healthy immune system.

The nutritional aspects of immunity have been studied for several decades, and it is clear that a well-nourished person is much more likely to mount a healthy immune response than one who is undernourished. In particular, the antioxidant system plays a key role. Ample levels of vitamins

E, C, A, and the carotenoids along with the minerals selenium, zinc, and copper are essential for responding to the inner and outer challenges to our well-being. For example, a recent study from Tufts University found that supplemental doses of vitamin E can improve the immunity of healthy subjects, at an optimal daily dose of 200 IU. Other studies looking at vitamin C and beta-carotene have also suggested that abundant levels of these antioxidants are important for optimal immunity.

Nutrients on the Horizon

As interest in the role of nutrition in health expands, we are seeing a number of new substances coming to market with the promise that they can reverse aging while improving health and vitality. Most of these claims are based on limited studies that are intriguing but not conclusive. It may turn out that some of these nutraceuticals have real value, but we believe it is too soon to justify their routine inclusion in our nutritional program. In this section we review a variety of these "horizon" substances and encourage you to research them yourself before adding them to your nutritional program.

S-Adenosyl-Methionine (SAMe)

SAMe is a natural compound that your body manufactures from the amino acid methionine. It is involved in many essential metabolic reactions including the production of key brain chemicals. Studies on people with depression have suggested that at supplemental doses of 1,600 milligrams per day, over 60 percent will show improvement in their mood, often within one to two weeks.

SAMe has only been available in the United States for a few years and remains expensive. It is usually sold in 200-milligram tablets that can cost more than $2.50 per pill, so a standard dose may cost $20 per day. Side effects tend to be mild but may include nausea, headaches, weakness, and rare palpitations. Some SAMe advocates discourage its use in bipolar disorder, suggesting that it can aggravate the manic phase. It has been used in lower doses of 800 milligrams per day to treat fibromyalgia. It is often recommended that SAMe be taken along with vitamins B6, B12, and folic acid to enhance its efficacy.

SAMe may be an effective alternative to antidepressant medications, but we believe that more scientific research is necessary before we can recommend its routine use. If you are feeling persistently sad and depleted, please see your health-care provider to discuss all potentially helpful treatment options, including SAMe.

Growth Hormone

In 1990 an intriguing article on aging by Dr. Daniel Rudman and his colleagues appeared in the *New England Journal of Medicine.* Men between sixty and eighty years of age were given human growth hormone (hGH) injections three times a week for six months. At the completion of the study, the men who had received hGH shots had an increase in their lean body mass, a decrease in their fat content, and an increase in the thickness of their skin. Initially, these results were enthusiastically advertised as evidence that hGH was the sought-after fountain of youth. Unfortunately, subsequent reports found that several undesirable side effects developed with its ongoing use. Growth hormone injections had to be discontinued in a number of men due to the development of carpal tunnel syndrome, edema, joint aches, or breast swelling. Other reports found that although a person developed greater muscle mass on hGH, they did not increase their strength. In fact, adding growth hormone to an good exercise program did not add additional benefit.

Due to the high cost and inconvenience of hGH injections, there have been attempts to stimulate the production and release of growth hormone through amino acids taken orally. It has been known for many years that giving the amino acid arginine intravenously increases the level of growth hormone. Efforts to boost growth hormone levels with oral arginine have met with mixed results. Considering all the currently available information, we do not believe that there is enough current evidence to support the long-term value of pharmacologically manipulating growth hormone levels. We will continue to follow the research in this area with great interest.

Dehydroepiandrosterone (DHEA)

This natural hormone produced by the adrenal glands must have a purpose, but despite the fact that it was identified over fifty years ago, scientists have not yet determined what it does. It is known that we make very little DHEA during the first ten years of life, we make a lot of it between the ages of twenty and forty, and then we gradually discontinue making it, so by the time we are seventy, we have less DHEA than we had as teenagers. The effects of giving animals and people supplementary DHEA have yielded contradictory results, generating a lot of controversy. Some enthusiastic advocates promote DHEA as *the* antiaging elixir, while most medical scientists believe that further study is necessary to determine its lasting benefits and risks to health. Among the thousands of studies on this intriguing chemical, there are reports that it can relieve depression, improve certain aspects of memory, reduce body fat, and enhance immunity. In a recent study from France, men and women between the ages of sixty and eighty years were given a daily DHEA dose of 50 milligrams and compared to other subjects taking a placebo. At the conclusion of the one-year experiment, mild benefits to the skin were seen in the younger men, while women over seventy showed modest improvements in their skin, bones, and libido. Whether these effects are due to the conversion of DHEA to male and female sex hormones or a specific action of DHEA on its own is not known. Unfortunately, for almost every study that suggests a benefit there is usually another one that fails to support it.

Although serious side effects are uncommon, DHEA is converted into male and female hormones and may contribute to health concerns ranging from acne to activation of breast and prostate cancer to psychiatric problems. The other issue of concern with DHEA is that we really don't know what long-term side effects it may cause. Although the recent French study lasted a year, most investigations showing either benefit or no benefit have lasted less than three months. We believe that too many questions still need to be answered before we can endorse the routine use of this fascinating hormone. We'll continue to watch DHEA with great interest and provide you with updates as new information unfolds. In the meantime, we can take some reassurance from a study which showed that regular practitioners of meditation have higher DHEA levels than people who are not meditating.

Phenolic Compounds

Nutritional scientists have identified many health-enhancing substances that come from our food. Members of the natural plant chemical family known as phenolic compounds are receiving a lot of attention for their potent antioxidant properties. Some of the chemicals that you may have heard about include bioflavonoids, isoflavonoids, catechins, and proanthocyanidins. Found in green tea, berries, grape skins and seeds, as well as pine bark, some of these natural chemicals have been found to be as much as fifty times more powerful scavengers of free radicals than vitamins C and E. The antioxidant properties of the proanthocyanidins derived from grapes may explain the beneficial effect of wine on the heart. In addition to a possible role in the prevention of heart disease, these substances have also been shown to have possible protective activity against cancer, degenerative brain conditions, and macular degeneration of the eye.

As a result of these studies, many nutritional supplement companies are offering concentrated capsules of these helpful agents. Grape seed extract, powdered green tea extract, and pine bark extract (commonly known as pycnogenol) are widely available in health food stores and have been promoted as antiaging wonder drugs. We agree that these substances are natural botanical gifts, but believe they are best consumed as nature provided them. Our bottom line regarding these super antioxidants is to eat plenty of blueberries, strawberries, raspberries, blackberries, and cranberries. Consume lots of grapes and chew the seeds. A cup or two of green tea will invigorate you while you are receiving the antioxidant benefits of the polyphenols contained within. In regards to this class of age-reversing allies, we believe that good food is better than good medicine.

Our Daily Vitamin Recommendations

Living beings have evolved for billions of years without the consumption of nutritional supplements, with most of the substances packed into a multivitamin tablet having been identified chemically only within the last century. And yet it is becoming increasingly clear that the levels of vitamins that prevent a deficiency disease may not be the levels that provide optimal health. We view nutritional supplementation as an insurance policy. The following daily doses are encouraged to complement a well-balanced diet. They fall well within safety limits while reflecting the information on the role that higher intake may play in lowering the risk for the common conditions that deplete our vitality and make us sick. You can usually fulfill these requirements by taking a high-potency multivitamin, multimineral supplement. Our recommended Reversal of Aging nutritional complement plan is listed in the appendix.

If you are at risk for heart disease, you may benefit from an additional dose of B vitamins, including folic acid, B6, and B12. If you feel

NUTRIENT	OUR RECOMMENDATIONS	% RECOMMENDATION ALLOWANCE
VITAMINS		
B1 (Thiamin)	7.5 mg	500
B2 (Riboflavin)	8.5 mg	500
Niacin (Niacinamide)	100 mg	500
B6 (Pyridoxine)	10 mg	500
Folic acid	400 mcg	100
B12 (Cobalamin)	30 mcg	500
Biotin	300 mcg	100
Pantothenic acid	50 mg	500
C (Ascorbic acid)	500 mg	833
A (Beta-carotene)	10,000 IU (½ from vitamin A, ½ from beta-carotene)	200
D (Calciferols)	400 IU	100
E (Tocopherols)	400 IU	1333
ESSENTIAL MINERALS		
Calcium	1000–1500 mg	100
Magnesium	400 mg	100
Iodine	150 mcg	100
Zinc	15 mg	100
Selenium	200 mcg	285
Copper	2 mg	100
Manganese	2 mg	100
Chromium	125 mcg	100
Molybdenum	83 mcg	100
Boron	1 mg	Not yet established

your memory is not serving you as well as you remember it did, consider adding a daily helping of ginkgo biloba. If your joints have been calling for attention, increase your intake of omega-3 fatty acids and try supplementing with glucosamine sulfate. Using these concentrated nutrients to complement a healthy lifestyle and diet can help you grow younger and live longer. But do not forget: *Nutritional supplements are not a substitute for a nutritionally balanced diet.*

Nutrient Ritual

Rituals serve to focus your attention. You probably cannot remember what you wore to dinner last Thursday evening, but if that night you attended an awards ceremony or a birthday celebration, the previously forgotten details may become available to you. Rituals take you from mindlessness to mindfulness. They bring you into present moment awareness. Rituals focus your intentions and stimulate your inner drugstore to produce age-reversing compounds.

Consciously taking your supplements can empower their effects and enhance their benefits. Although some disparage the so-called placebo effect, we see it as a valuable expression of your natural inherent health-promoting pharmacy. When you anticipate the benefits of nutritional complements, you activate your body's rejuvenating chemicals to work in partnership with them.

Each morning when you take your nutrients, spend a few moments acknowledging the rejuvenating, strengthening, and life-enhancing influence they are having on you. Envision the subtle yet potent nourishment these vital nutrients are providing every cell, tissue, and organ in your body. Make the process of taking your nutritional complements a daily health-promoting ritual. Repeat the affirmations that reinforce your Biostat while taking your nutrients. Use your attention and intention to augment their age-reversing power. As you are taking your nutritional complements, repeat:

Every day in every way, I am increasing
my mental and physical capacity.
My Biostat is set at a healthy ____ years of age.
I look and feel a healthy ____ years old.

I am reversing my biological age:

- *By changing my perception of my body, its aging and time;*

- *Through two kinds of deep rest—restful awareness and restful sleep;*
- *By nurturing my body through healthy foods; and*
- *By using nutritional complements wisely.*

6

You Can Reverse Your Biological Age by Enhancing Mind/Body Integration

ACTION STEP #5

I am reversing my biological age by enhancing mind/body integration.

I put this into practice by:

1. *Performing breathing techniques (Pranayama) five to ten minutes daily.*
2. *Performing ten to fifteen minutes of yoga, tai chi, or qigong each day.*
3. *Practicing body awareness and learning to follow the healthy signals from my body when there are conflicting messages from my mind.*

The body and mind are one.
When the intimate relationship
between mind and body is disrupted,
aging and entropy accelerate.
Restoring mind/body integration
brings about renewal.
Through conscious breathing
and movement techniques,
you can renew the body/mind
and reverse the aging process.

You can reverse your biological age by enhancing the integration between your mind and body. Mind and body are intimately interconnected. Your body is composed of physiological systems, organs, and tissues, but at its basis is a collection of molecules. Your mind is composed of ideas and beliefs, memories and desires, but is essentially a collection of thoughts. Your body is a molecular field; your mind is a thought field. Giving rise to both your field of molecules and your field of thoughts is an underlying field of consciousness, which is the source of both your mind and body. Every time you have a thought you precipitate a molecule in your nervous system that influences the other molecules throughout your body. Stagnation in the mind/body connection results in aging and illness. Enlivening the mind/body connection leads to healing and the reversal of aging.

Enhancing the integration between mind and body requires listening to the signals from inside as attentively as you listen to information from the outside. Mind/body integration means establishing a healthy dialogue between your thoughts and molecules. It means listening to your body and responding with love and reverence. A body listened to answers back with energy, strength, and flexibility—the qualities of a body growing younger.

There are many established practices devoted to enhancing mind/body integration. Yoga, tai chi, qigong, akaido, and other disciplines use conscious breathing and physical movements to bring your attention into the body and into the present moment. These approaches enable you to listen to the signals your body is sending and to enliven energy in the body through your attention and intention.

There is an expression in the Bhagavad Gita, the ancient Vedic epic, that in Sanskrit goes *"Yogastah kuru karmani."* This can be translated into English as "Established in yoga, perform action." Yoga here means union. The English word *yoke,* as in "uniting two oxen," is related to this Sanskrit root. Established in yoga, then, means established in a state of unity in which body, mind, and spirit are experienced as one continuum. Once your consciousness is on this level, you perform your daily actions without losing your connection to wholeness.

This is the goal of all mind/body integration techniques.

Breathing Integration

Conscious breath work is at the center of mind/body integration. The breath integrates mind and body. Thought is the movement of breath. Breath is the movement of thought. When your mind is agitated, your breathing is disturbed. When your mind is serene, your breathing is calm. You can use mental techniques to calm your breath, as in meditation. Likewise, you can use breathing techniques to calm your mind. In yoga and Ayurveda, these breathing techniques are called *Pranayama.* The word means "expanding Prana," or "expansion of the life force."

There are Pranayama practices to energize you, soothe your body, and quiet your mind. Depending on the technique and your intention, you can use Pranayama to enliven you in the morning, calm you when you are upset, or settle your mind when you are trying to go to sleep. Let's review three basic conscious breathing exercises to enhance your mind/body integration and reverse aging.

Energizing Breath

You can invigorate your body and mind with the breathing technique known as *bhastrika* or "bellows breath." This exercise cleanses your lungs while increasing the oxygen flow to your cells and tissues.

Sit comfortably with your spine upright and close your eyes. Exhale all the air from your lungs. Then begin deep in-and-out breathing through your nose silently using the mantras "So" on the inflow and "Hum" on the outflow. For the first twenty breaths take two-second slow forceful inhalations and two-second slow forceful exhalations. It is easiest to keep track of the number of breaths by counting on your fingers.

The next twenty breaths are performed faster with approximately one-second inhalations and one-second exhalations. These are also performed through the nose while thinking "So" on the in-breath and "Hum" on the out-breath.

Finally, perform twenty rapid bhastrika breaths, with approximately half-second inhalations and half-second exhalations. After the twenty rapid breaths, perform one more slow deep breath and then simply feel the sensations in your body. You will notice that your mind is clear and quiet while your body is energized.

Do not hyperventilate to the point where you are feeling lightheaded or dizzy. The breath movement is almost entirely abdominal, using your diaphragm to move air. Your head and shoulders should be relaxed and mostly still. Use bhastrika when you are feeling a little sluggish and need a quick replenishment of energy. It is also beneficial prior to your afternoon meditation to clear away drowsiness before you start your practice.

Soothing Breath

The soothing breath technique known as *Ujayi* can be used to settle your mind and body when you are feeling frustrated or irritated. When performed correctly it creates a cooling effect at the back of the throat and has a stabilizing influence on the cardiorespiratory system.

To perform Ujayi breath, take a slightly deeper than normal inhalation. On the exhalation, slightly constrict your throat muscles so it sounds as if you are snoring. Your out-breath is through your nose with your mouth closed. Another way to get the hang of this practice is to first exhale, "Haaah," with your mouth open. Now make a similar motion with your mouth closed. This will result in the desired breathy, snoring sound.

Once you have mastered it on the outflow, perform the same procedure on inflow. The result is that you sound a little like Darth Vader from *Star Wars.*

When you find yourself becoming aggravated or upset, shift into Ujayi breath and you will notice a prompt soothing influence. You can also use this when performing yoga postures and while exercising at a moderate level. Practicing this soothing breath technique will reduce wear and tear on your physiology and slow aging.

Relaxing Breath

You can calm your mind with the breathing technique known as *Nadi Shodhana.* In English this means, "clearing the channels." Nadi Shodhana is very beneficial when you are having a lot of anxious thoughts, and when you are trying to quiet your mind. It requires the use of your right hand to alternately close your right, then left nostril. Hold your hand so your thumb, index finger, and remaining fingers are separated. You use your thumb to close your right nostril and your third and fourth finger to close your left.

Take a slow moderately deep breath, and then close off your right nasal passage with your thumb. Exhale slowly through your left nostril, then inhale slowly through your left nostril, then close off your left nostril with your third and fourth fingers. Exhale through your right nostril, inhale through your right nostril, and then again close your right nasal passage, exhaling through your left. Continue with this pattern for five to ten minutes, alternating the nostril after each inhalation. After just a few cycles you will experience your mind calming and your body relaxing.

Nadi Shodhana

Use these practices throughout the day to balance your mind and body. Pranayama can energize you without the need for caffeine, relax you without the need for tranquilizers, and soothe you without the need for alcohol. These natural techniques help to balance and nourish the field of energy, transformation, and intelligence commonly known as your body/mind.

Mind/Body Movement

Techniques such as yoga, tai chi, and qigong can be thought of as practice sessions for establishing yourself in a state of body/mind/spirit unity while engaging in action. Each of these ancient practices enlivens the integration between body and mind.

Reversal-of-Aging Yoga

It is a rare town in the Western world in which you cannot find a yoga class. This would not have been the case twenty-five years ago, when the average Westerner's vision of a yoga practitioner was an emaciated, loinclothed man on a bed of nails. Today, yoga has gone mainstream with classes available in shopping malls, YMCAs, and corporate fitness clubs. Yoga can help enliven many aspects of mind/body fitness, serving to enhance relaxation, flexibility, muscle tone, and strength.

The roots of yoga go back at least five thousand years, a testament to its enduring value, independent of time or culture. Modern science has recently begun to pay attention to the measurable benefits of yoga in a variety of health domains including arthritis, asthma, heart disease, and diabetes. Most people do yoga because it helps them become centered and relaxed while enhancing the comfort they experience in their bodies.

There are hundreds of different yoga systems available in the world today. Some are designed to build strength; others are intended more for flexibility and relaxation. Regardless of the system you are attracted to, be certain to perform your postures with full awareness in your body, heeding the signals of comfort and discomfort that are generated. Practice your poses regularly and consciously and you will see steady improvement in your flexibility and mind/body integration.

The Sun Salutations

A set of twelve yoga positions known as the Sun Salutations are a wonderful, balanced series of movements that can enhance flexibility, strength, and even aerobic capacity, depending upon how they are performed. We recommend moving through a few rounds of the Sun Salutations at least once a day, either early in the morning or in the late afternoon, when the sun is rising or setting. They provide a full stretch to all the key areas of the body and awaken our intrinsic vitality.

1. Salutation pose

1. Stand with your feet firmly on the ground, eyes facing forward, with the palms of your hands held together in front of your chest. Breathe slowly and evenly with your attention in your body.

2. Sky-reaching pose

2. Tightening the muscles in your buttocks, reach upward with both arms, looking toward the sky, while at the same time elongating your spine. Inhale as your perform this posture.

3. Hands/feet pose

3. Slowly flex your body forward from your hips, relaxing your spine as you bring your hands down alongside your feet. Relax your neck muscles and bend your knees if necessary to place your hand on the floor. Exhale during this pose.

4. Equestrian pose

4. Stretch your left leg backward, bending your right knee until you are resting on the left

knee and toes of your left foot. At the same time, open your chest as you look forward. Inhale as you stretch back and up.

5. Mountain pose

5. Bring your left leg back even with your right and raise your buttocks, with straight legs and arms. Stretch your heels toward the floor, lengthening the back of your legs as your body forms a tent. Exhale during this pose.

6. Eight limbs pose

6. Gently lower yourself so your forehead, chest, and knees are touching the floor while you maintain the bulk of your weight on your toes and fingers. Breathe easily in and out during this posture.

7. Cobra pose

7. Allow your weight to rest on your pelvis while you lift your chest off the ground, gently arching your back. At first, lift only with the muscles of the back. After you are comfortable, gently push up with your hands, but *do not overarch.* Inhale during this pose.

The final five poses repeat postures 1 through 5 in reverse order.

8. Mountain pose

8. Return to this pose by again raising your buttocks in the air while you exhale.

9. Equestrian pose

9. Bring your left leg forward, bending your left knee, leaving your right leg extended behind you, inhaling while you open your chest.

10. Hands/feet pose

10. Bring your right foot forward even with your left as you raise your buttocks, keeping both hands on the floor beside your feet.

Bend your knees as you need to while exhaling.

11. Sky-reaching pose

11. Slowly raise your body, leading with your hands until you are stretching toward the sky; inhale as you straighten your spine.

12. Salutation pose

12. Once again return to this resting pose with your palms together in front of your chest, breathing easily.

These twelve postures constitute one cycle. Do between four and twelve rounds at a time. Done vigorously, they can raise your heart rate and provide a cardiovascular workout. Performed in a slow, relaxed manner, they will have a calming effect on your body and mind. Try using the Ujayi breath as you are inhaling and exhaling during the poses. Keep your attention in your body, releasing any tension or resistance you may feel. Listen to your body's signals while performing the poses for the optimal age-reversing mind/body integration.

Sitting Sun Salutes

You can perform a sitting variation of the twelve Sun Salutations with almost the same benefit as doing them on the floor. They can be done at work in your office chair or in an airplane seat. They will stretch and tone you while increasing your circulation.

1. Sit comfortably on a firm chair with your feet resting solidly on the floor. With your palms together in front of your chest, center your awareness in your body, breathing easily.

2. Reach your arms upward, stretching your shoulders and upper back while you inhale.

3. Bend forward, relaxing your spine until your palms are on the floor next to your feet. Rest your chest on your thighs as you relax your neck, exhaling.

4. Raise your body up and grasp your right knee with interlaced fingers. Straighten and arch your back as you extend your arms, inhaling.

5. Flex your hip, bringing your knee up to your chest, while you roll your shoulders, upper back, and neck forward. Partially exhale.

6. Releasing your leg, return both feet to the floor and again bend forward with your palms on the floor and your chest resting on your knees. Fully exhale.

7. With your fingertips dangling on or near the floor, raise your head and arch your neck and upper back, partially inhaling.

8. Again raise your body, this time grasping your left knee with your interlaced fingers. Arch your back as you apply downward pressure with your knee, stretching your arms. Inhale.

9. Again, flex your hip as you bring your knee to your chest, partially exhaling.

10. For the third time, bend fully forward, placing your palms on the floor next to your feet. Exhale fully.

11. Raise your chest fully upward, leading with your arms, until you are stretching toward the sky. Fully inhale.

12. Return to the original pose with your hands at your chest; feel the sensations in your body with your full attention, breathing easily.

Reversal-of-Aging Tai Chi and Qigong

The mind/body techniques of tai chi and qigong are centuries old. Their graceful slow movements improve balance, flexibility, and strength, enhancing both mental and physical well-being. Qi (chi) is the Chinese word for life force. Tai chi is the process of connecting with the supreme universal force. Qigong is translated as "energy cultivation." Both techniques are closely related meditations in motion, designed to awaken awareness in the body with their fluid, centered movements. Millions of people perform tai chi and qigong in China where they are considered premier mind/body fitness programs that cultivate relaxation in the midst of action. They integrate intention, breath, and movement to enhance mind/body coordination.

Scientific studies on these practices have documented many benefits on several aspects of health. People practicing tai chi show improved balance and coordination as well as enhanced heart and lung fitness. We encourage you to find a local tai chi or qigong class and use these beautiful movements to awaken mind/body integration.

To get a sense of the calming vitality these techniques provide, try this simple basic movement.

Moving Your Energy

Perform this beginning movement with your full attention in your body. All the moves are continuous, fluid, and in slow motion.

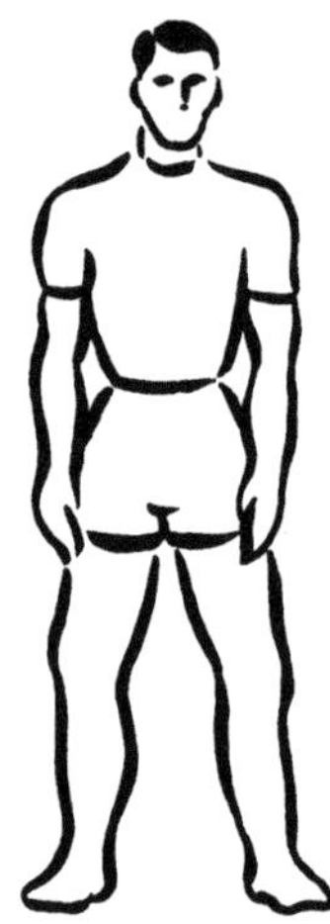

1. Stand with your feet a little more than shoulder-width apart, parallel to each other.

2. Slowly raise your arms forward and upward, while at the same time slightly bending your

knees. Continue until your hands are about shoulder height, with your fingertips pointing toward each other about six inches apart, your palms facing toward you.

3. Continue moving slowly as you rotate your shoulder inward, lowering your hands so your palms face the floor at about waist height. At the same time, bend your knees a little more.

4. Again, gradually raise your arms and hands until your fingertips are again facing each other; at the same time, rise up slightly, partially straightening your knees.

5. Repeat this sequence several times, imagining that you are moving in water. After a few cycles, slowly lower your hands to your side and resume a normal relaxed stance.

Consciousness in Motion

Each of these mind/body practices encourages the body to express its natural vitality through movement. As the energy of your body is allowed to flow, the chattering of your mind subsides and a state of innocent witnessing emerges. This experience of being fully present in your body cultivates mind/body integration, enhancing the sensitivity of your thoughts to your molecules.

Just as we know that our thoughts and feelings can influence our body, we know that our bodies influence our psychology and emotions. Changing your posture, pose, or position has a direct and immediate influence on how you feel and think. If you are feeling depleted and exhausted, try changing the way you are sitting or standing to reflect a more energized position and notice how your mental state is transformed. Developing enhanced mind/body integration through yoga, tai chi, and qigong allows imbalances to be identified and corrected more readily, before they create more established conditions.

We encourage you to find your program of conscious movement. Practicing these procedures with your full attention will enable you to maintain a clear and healthy line of communication between your mind and body at all stages of your life.

Mind/Body Communication

Not listening to your body's healthy signals accelerates aging and is the root cause of many illnesses. When your body is expressing a healthy need but your mind refuses to listen, imbalances begin, and the seeds of mind/body *disintegration* are sown. Here are several common examples of mind/body communication breakdown:

- Your body is tired and needs to sleep; your mind overrides this need in order to watch a late-night television show.
- Your body is full at the end of a meal; your mind insists on returning to the buffet for another helping of dessert.
- Your body needs to eat; your mind insists that you have to work through lunch.
- Your body is calling you to empty your bladder; your mind refuses to leave your seat in the middle of a movie.
- Your body is asking to stretch; your mind refuses to disturb the other passengers in your airplane row.

Start listening to the signals from your body and honoring those that are health-promoting. You know which signals are good for you and which come from unhealthy habits. Whenever there is a conflict between your physical needs and your mental or emotional ones, ask yourself a simple question: Will fulfilling this need help me grow younger and live longer? If the answer is yes, fulfill the need. If the answer is no, because you recognize that the behavior is potentially harmful, pass. If due to a habit or addiction, the impulse is so strong that it overrides your better judgment, perform the action with full awareness and attention in your body. Consciously witness your choice without harshly judging yourself. If you are meditating regularly and are witnessing your choices, you will soon find that fewer impulses arise to create conflict between your mind and body.

Every day in every way,
I am increasing my mental and physical capacity.
My Biostat is set at a healthy ____ years of age.
I look and feel a healthy ____ years old.

I am reversing my biological age:

- *By changing my perception of my body, its aging, and time;*
- *Through two kinds of deep rest—restful awareness and restful sleep;*
- *By nurturing my body through healthy foods;*
- *By using nutritional complements wisely; and*
- *By enhancing mind/body integration.*

7

You Can Reverse Your Biological Age Through Exercise

ACTION STEP #6

I am reversing my biological age through regular exercise.

I put this into practice by:

1. *Performing some aerobic activity at least three times a week.*
2. *Performing twenty minutes of strength training at least three times a week.*
3. *Consciously making choices that keep me physically active.*

A complete exercise program includes attention to stretching, strength training, and cardiovascular conditioning. Exercise reverses all the biomarkers of aging.

One of the most important steps to reverse your biological age is regular exercise. In this age of push-button technology you run the risk of spending so much time in your mind that you neglect the needs of your body. One of the critical needs of your body is to move. "Use it or lose it" is directly applicable to your physical body. We are seeing a growing epidemic of obesity in Western society that is now affecting our children, mainly because the average person—adult or child—spends less time moving their body than at any point in human history. As a result of not exercising regularly, we suffer increased risks for heart disease, high blood pressure, diabetes, arthritis, osteoporosis, and cancer.

Several studies have shown how hazardous inactivity can be to your health. A report published in 1968 found that if you impose bed rest on young, healthy men for three weeks, their measurements of cardiovascular fitness deteriorate by the equivalent of almost twenty years of aging. As anyone who has had to wear a cast for a broken bone knows firsthand, not using a muscle leads to wasting and weakness.

Exercise alone can alter many of the important biomarkers of aging. Drs. William Evans and Irwin Rosenberg from Tufts University have documented the powerful effects exercise has on improving muscle mass, strength, aerobic capacity, bone density, and many other key biological markers of aging. One of the most effective ways to raise your level of HDL cholesterol (the "good" cholesterol) is through exercise. Studies have shown that men sixty to seventy years old can increase their muscle strength by 100 to over 200 percent after just twelve weeks of training. While your body is getting stronger, it is also getting leaner. As a result, your ability to handle sugar is improved and the risks for diabetes are reduced. Regular weight training strengthens your bones and lessens the chances for developing osteoporosis. This is particularly important for women who are at risk of losing bone once they are beyond their reproductive years.

Of all the approaches to growing younger, exercise produces the most prompt returns. Within a week of beginning a fitness program, you'll notice definite improvement in your sense of well-being. After a few weeks you will not be able to go without it. Regular exercise is an essential element of the reversal-of-aging program.

Total Fitness

A complete fitness program includes exercises to enhance flexibility, strength, and endurance. Improving suppleness in the body improves your physical and emotional comfort level and reduces your chances for injury. As discussed in the last chapter, yoga, tai chi, and qigong all expand flexibility while enhancing mind/body integration. At least ten minutes of gentle, conscious stretching should be a part of every exercise warm-up routine. Unfortunately, we see too many people who have the good intention to start exercising, but fail to take the time to warm up properly. As a result, they strain a muscle or pull a ligament and are unable to continue the fitness program they need.

Building strength enhances vitality and reverses a common feature of aging known as *sarcopenia.* This word, coined by researchers at Tufts University, means "lack of flesh." Weakness, reduced muscle mass, and increased body fat are well-known consequences of inactivity. But they can all be reversed through strength training. Improving muscle tone through weight-bearing exercises can also improve your posture and reduce back pain. If you are dealing with chronic low-back problems and believe you cannot exercise, start slowly to build your back and abdominal muscle strength and your pain will diminish.

There are emotional and psychological benefits of exercise. Hundreds of studies attest to the value of regular exercise on your mood and mental state. These are some of the psychological benefits that have been shown with exercise:

- Less depression
- Less anxiety
- Less anger
- Less cynical distrust
- Improved self-esteem
- Better resilience to stress
- Improved sleep

Exercise gives you a greater sense of confidence and competence. It is good for your body and good for your mind. Let's look more closely at the essential ingredients of an effective age-reversing fitness program.

Flexibility

Perform a few minutes of stretching before a more vigorous strength-training or cardiovascular workout. Particularly if you have a sedentary job in which you are sitting for hours at a time, a few minutes of flexibility exercise will overcome the shortening and tightness of muscles that comes with inactivity. Surprisingly, there is only limited scientific documentation that stretching before exercise reduces muscle injuries. Those reports that show a benefit suggest that active stretching while holding a position for fifteen seconds provides the most benefit. If you are prone to low-back pain, spine-stretching exercises can reduce your discomfort during and after your exercise time.

Try five to ten minutes of yoga or another flexibility exercise each day at the start of your workout. The Sun Salutations (see page 155) stretch every muscle group, improve spinal flexibility, increase circulation, and improve muscle tone. Use the Sun Salutations to bring your attention into your body in preparation for strength training and aerobic activity.

Building Strength

Muscles respond to use, which means that to build strength you have to regularly activate a muscle group. The human body has over one hundred different muscles that govern your movements and support your posture. You can gain great benefit by systematically exercising the major muscle groups in your arms, legs, and trunk. The key to building muscle strength is to start off slowly and gradually build up your conditioning level. While fitness centers offer expanded exercise options and can provide needed motivation, you do not need expensive equipment to get a good workout.

The Basic Seven

Try the basic seven exercises below every other day for two weeks and you will see a noticeable improvement in your muscle tone and strength. Plan to spend four to five minutes performing each exercise for a thirty-minute strength-building workout.

1. Curls

1. Curls. This exercise builds the muscles that flex the elbow. Find an object that weighs four to five pounds to start. You can purchase a small dumbbell or use an unopened half-gallon container of water, milk, or orange juice. Sitting in a chair with your back supported, do ten to fifteen repetitions: Start with your forearm resting on your thigh, palm facing up. Slowly extend your elbow and then fully flex it. Inhale while flexing your arms and exhale while extending. After completing a round of repetitions, rest about half a minute and then repeat. Do this three to five times with each arm. After a few weeks, you can gradually increase the weight

by a couple of pounds. This exercise primarily strengthens the biceps muscle.

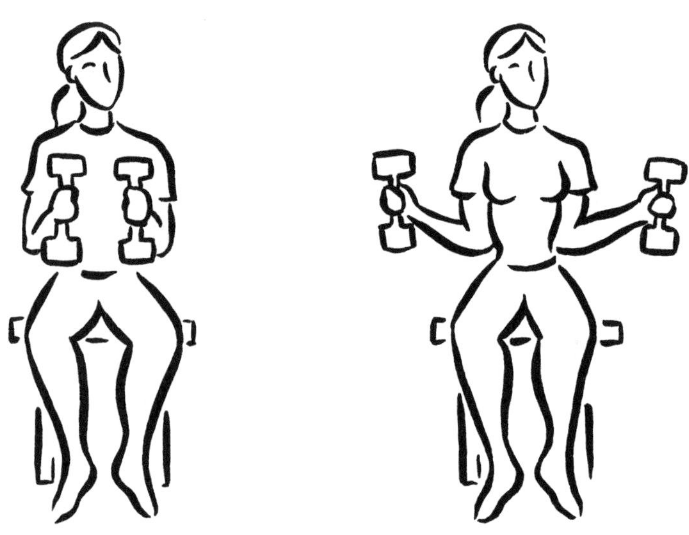

2. Shoulder rotators

2. Shoulder rotators. A valuable exercise that reduces shoulder injuries is one that strengthens the muscles that rotate your arms outward. Most exercise programs do not work these external rotators, creating imbalances in the shoulder girdle. These imbalances then predispose you to rotator cuff injuries.

   Sit with your back supported and use the same weight as above. With your elbows held at your sides, begin with your arms straight ahead and parallel to the floor. Now slowly rotate your hands outward as far as you can.

Hold this position for a few seconds and then return to the starting point. Repeat the external rotations ten times.

Another way to strengthen these same muscles is by using a large elastic rubber band that you hold with both hands. Then, rotate your arms externally using the rubber band for resistance.

3. Push-ups

3. Push-ups. This well-known exercise helps build the shoulder girdle muscles and the triceps. If you cannot do full straight-legged push-ups, begin with modified ones, supporting your weight on your knees. Inhale while

lowering yourself toward the floor and exhale while rising. Begin with eight to ten repetitions, resting for half a minute between sets. Aim for three sets the first week, gradually increasing to five.

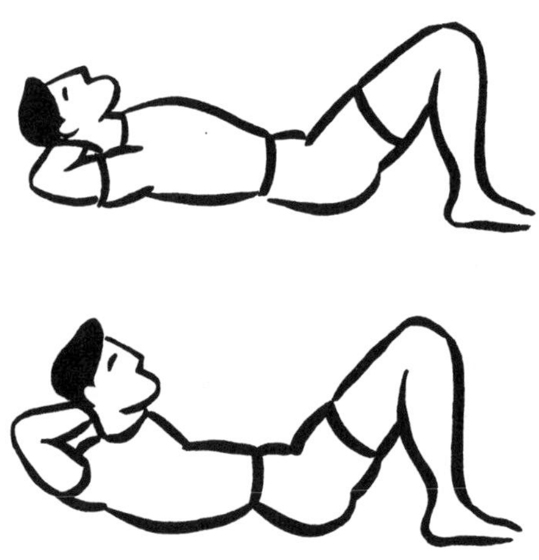

4. Abdominl crunches

4. Abdominal crunches. When doing abdominal crunches it is important to recognize that you need to raise your head only 25 to 30 degrees off the ground to gain maximum benefit. As opposed to sit-ups, abdominal crunches do not place unnecessary strain on your spine. Lie on a padded surface with your knees bent and your fingers laced behind your head. Lift your head and shoulders off the ground with your chin separated about a fist distance from your chest.

Inhale while lifting off and exhale while returning to the floor. Perform fifteen crunches, followed by half a minute of rest. Begin with three sets, gradually increasing to five.

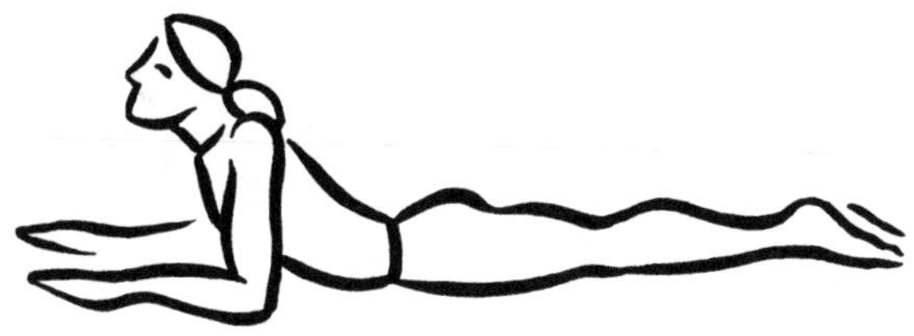

5. Back stengtheners

5. Back strengtheners. Lie on your stomach with your palms on the floor. *Without pushing off with your hands,* slowly lift your chest off the floor by tightening your back muscles. Your arms and hands are just used to provide stabilization. Repeatedly raise and lower your chest to the floor, using only your back muscles. Do about twenty to twenty-five lifts as a set.

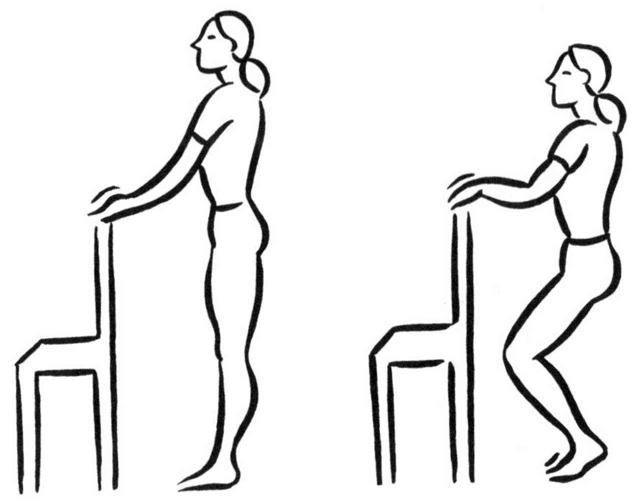

6. Thigh strengtheners

6. Thigh strengtheners. These are best performed while supporting yourself with your hands on a table or chair. To protect your knees and gain a full thigh muscle workout, do not bend beyond 90 degrees at the knees. Maintain your back perpendicular to the floor. Inhale while you are squatting and exhale while rising. Begin with fifteen squats, rest for half a minute and then repeat the set.

You can gain similar benefits by stair-stepping. Find a platform that is a foot off the ground and repeatedly step up, leading first with one leg, then the other. Start with twenty-five steps with each leg. Continue until you feel a mild burn in your thigh muscles.

You can also use weights to strengthen the muscles that extend your knee. Sit in a firm chair with your back supported; place a two- to five-pound weight around each ankle. Slowly straighten your knee, hold it for a few seconds, and then slowly return your foot to the floor. Do one side then the other, beginning with about ten repetitions.

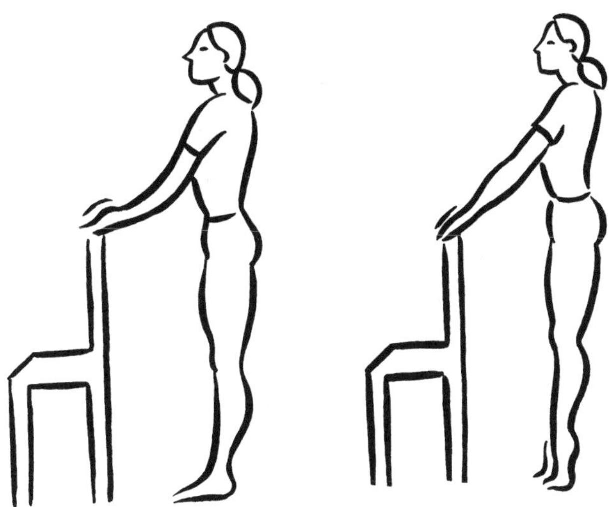

7. Toe risers

7. Toe risers. This exercise tones and strengthens the calf muscles. Stand in your bare or stocking feet, supporting yourself with your hands on a table or chair. Slowly raise your-

self up on your toes, and then slowly lower yourself. Inhale while you are rising and exhale while lowering. Do twenty to twenty-five raises, rest for half a minute and repeat. Try three sets at first, gradually increasing to five.

Circulating the Life Force

The human physiology is a sophisticated biological instrument designed to transform creativity into manifestation, thought into action. If you are not regularly increasing the flow of oxygen into your lungs and enhancing the circulation of blood through your body, you are not providing your physiology the opportunity to experience peak performance. As a result of inadequately exercising your cardiovascular and respiratory systems, you place yourself at increased risk for heart disease, high blood pressure, and a variety of different cancers. At any age and regardless of your current level of fitness, beginning an aerobic exercise program will improve your physical and emotional well-being and help you grow younger.

As is true with strength training, a cardiovascular fitness program does not have to be complicated in order to provide health-enhancing benefits. You do have to be regular, for your mind can always come up with some reason why exercise is not a good idea today, particularly if you get off your routine and miss a few sessions. Find an aerobic activity that you can do regularly—regardless of the weather—and stick with it. Three to four sessions per week for twenty to thirty minutes is usually enough to gain substantial benefits. There are a few simple principles to follow to determine how much and how often you should be exercising in order to gain maximum cardiovascular benefit.

Calculating Your Target Exercise Level

The first step is to calculate your maximal heart rate (MHR), which is determined by subtracting your age from 220.

220 –	________________	=	________________
	Your age in years		Maximal heart rate

For example, if you are 50 years old, your maximal heart rate is 170 (220–50). If you are just beginning an exercise program, first check with your health provider to make certain there are no contraindications to starting an unsupervised exercise program, such as heart disease, severe obesity, or limiting arthritis.

At the beginning of your program, aim to reach a target exercise heart rate between 50 and 60 percent of your MHR. Choose 60 percent if you are in reasonably good shape and 50 percent if you are not or if it's been a long time since you've performed any cardiovascular activity.

________________ × 0.6 = ________________

Maximal heart rate   Target heart rate

At age fifty, this is calculated to be 85 to 102 beats per minute (50% of 170 = 85; 60% of 170 = 102).

Take your pulse before you start and then begin exercising until your heart rate hits the target number. There are many high-quality heart monitors available for under $100 in the marketplace, with some as low as $50. If you do not have a monitoring device, you can still check your pulse every five to ten minutes while exercising, but it is easier to determine your exercise level if you can just glance at a wrist monitor.

Optimal benefit is gained when you exercise between twenty and thirty minutes, but if you are out of shape, begin with just ten or fifteen minutes. A wide range of activities can provide an effective cardiovascular workout, including jogging, bicycling, dancing, cycling, kickboxing, spinning, treadmill, stair-climbing, rowing, hiking, and swimming. Find something you like to do that is easily accessible to you. There is also proven benefit to cross-training. This means finding a few different strength-training and aerobic activities that you can rotate through on different days. One day you might use a treadmill for twenty minutes, the next day you may ride a bike, and another you may go to an aerobics dance class. Each activity will work a different set of muscles while improving your cardiovascular fitness. Establish a regular time for your daily routine to maintain consistency.

Once you are comfortable at your current level of activity, try gradually increasing your target heart rate from 65 to 75 percent of your MHR. At age fifty, this would mean a target heart between 110 and 128 beats per minute (65% of 170 = 110; 75% of 170 = 128). For the first couple of weeks, remain at 60 percent and then gradually increase your target rate by 5 percent every few weeks until you are at 70 to 75 percent of your MHR.

Do not increase your target rate if you are straining at your current level. You should be able to speak while you are exercising, although if you can easily carry on a conversation, you are probably ready to increase your intensity. For the most part, you should be able to breathe through your nose. Try thinking the "So Hum" mantra while you are exercising to keep your attention fully in your body, using "So" on inhalations and "Hum" on exhalations.

A thin layer of perspiration tells you that your body is burning calories, but you should not be sweating profusely. If at any time you become acutely short of breath or develop chest discomfort, stop your activity and immediately contact your health care provider. Although you will feel that you have definitely expended energy during a good workout, you should not feel completely exhausted or depleted. Some mild soreness is common at first or when you increase your intensity, but you should not have severe discomfort. Use common sense and aim for the long-term balanced benefits of a regular exercise program.

It will not take long to see improvements in both strength and cardiovascular fitness with a consistent fitness program. In addition to an improvement in your general sense of well-being, you will notice that you are losing accumulated weight, sleeping better, and experiencing better digestion and elimination. Most important, you will look and feel your healthy Biostat age. No one can take this step toward improved physical capacity but you. Start today and you will quickly see yourself growing younger.

Exercise on the Road

If your life involves a good deal of travel it will take some extra attention to stay on your exercise routine. Most hotels have a workout room with basic equipment. Ask about the exercise facilities when you are making a reservation. Even if equipment is not available, you can perform the basic seven exercises in your hotel room using two-liter water bottles for your weights. The other strength-training drills simply use your body.

If a treadmill is unavailable, you can get in your cardiovascular conditioning by doing Sun Salutations rapidly for fifteen to twenty minutes. Use the stairs instead of the hotel elevator to get to your room floor. If your business meeting is within walking distance, leave enough time to get there with a brisk stroll rather than taking a taxi. It is always easier to continue exercising regularly than it is to stop for a week or two and then restart. Make your fitness program a high priority. (For more information on the Grow Younger, Live Longer Fitness Program, see the appendix on page 379.)

Staying Active

Seek out opportunities during the day to be physically active. If you live half a mile from your fitness club, put on your running shoes and jog there instead of driving and spending ten minutes looking for a parking place. If you work on the twentieth story of a high-rise office building, take the elevator to the sixteenth floor and walk up the remaining flights of stairs. If you need to pick up a few items at the grocery store, ride your bike and save some fossil fuel. Park your car a few blocks from work and walk the rest of the way to and from your office.

Consciously make the choices to stay physically active. Your body and mind will respond with greater energy and vitality. Staying active will help you grow younger and live longer.

Every day in every way,
I am increasing my mental and physical capacity.
My Biostat is set at a healthy ____ years of age.
I look and feel a healthy ____ years old.

I am reversing my biological age:

- *By changing my perception of my body, its aging and time;*

- *Through two kinds of deep rest—restful awareness and restful sleep;*
- *By nurturing my body through healthy foods;*
- *By using nutritional complements wisely;*
- *By enhancing mind/body integration; and*
- *Through exercise.*

8

You Can Reverse Your Biological Age by Eliminating Toxins from Your Life

ACTION STEP #7

I am reversing my biological age by eliminating toxins from my physical and emotional bodies.

I put this into practice by:

1. *Eliminating all toxicity from my diet and drinking two to three liters of water every day.*
2. *Learning to handle emotional turbulence.*
3. *Healing or eliminating toxic relationships.*

The accumulation of toxins
in the body/mind system
accelerates aging.
The elimination of toxins
awakens the capacity for renewal.
Toxins must be identified and
eliminated from your
body, mind, and soul.

You can reverse your biological age by eliminating toxins from your life. Every impulse of life can be considered in terms of whether it brings nourishment or toxicity. A nourishing experience brings you happiness, expands your awareness, and helps you grow younger. A toxic experience brings misery, makes you feel stuck, and accelerates aging. This is true whether you are talking about toxic substances, toxic food, toxic relationships, or toxic emotions. An essential step to reverse the aging process is to identify and release toxins from every level of your life.

Aging and illness result from the accumulation of toxic reactions. Scientists now understand that toxic damage to cells and tissues is the consequence of free radicals that are formed whenever oxygen is metabolized. A free radical molecule is an oxygen molecule that is missing an electron. Also known as reactive oxygen species (ROS), they go by names such as hydroxy radical, singlet oxygen, superoxide, and hydrogen peroxide. These hungry chemicals are indiscriminate about how they replace their missing electron, and will strip one from any nearby source, including proteins, fats, or DNA molecules. Under controlled situations, free radicals are useful in metabolizing food and mounting an immune response against invading bacteria. However, the collateral damage of free radical formation is responsible for illness and aging. Many of the most common illnesses of our society linked to free radical damage are:

- Cancer
- Heart disease
- Stroke
- Diabetes
- Arthritis
- Osteoporosis
- Inflammatory bowel disease
- Glaucoma
- Retinal degeneration
- Alzheimer's disease

Wrinkling skin, graying hair, and stiffening joints are also the result of free radicals. There are things you can do that increase free radical production and other things that can limit them. Things that increase free radical formation include:

- Smoking
- Environmental pollution
- Alcohol
- Radiation, including excessive sunlight exposure
- Barbecued and smoked meats
- Aged and fermented foods
- Chemotherapy drugs
- High intake of saturated and hydrogenated fats
- Stress and stress hormones

We have evolved a sophisticated system to neutralize the damaging effects of free radicals on our bodies. This is called the *antioxidant system* and it involves many different enzymes, vitamins, and minerals. When your antioxidant system is fully operational, you are able to deactivate the free radical molecules before they do harm.

Things you can do to enhance your antioxidant system include:

- Eat more antioxidant-rich foods—fresh fruits, vegetables, grains, nuts, and beans.
- Use antioxidant-rich herbs and spices liberally—dill, coriander, rosemary, sage, thyme, mint, fennel, ginger, and garlic.
- Take antioxidant vitamins—A, C, and E.

- Eliminate tobacco, excessive alcohol, and nonessential drugs.
- Reduce your stress—meditate.

The accumulation of toxins in the body/mind system accelerates aging.

Relinquishing Toxic Substances

Human beings have this curious propensity to be attracted to things that are not good for them. Part of this affinity is chemical, for nicotine, illicit drugs, and alcohol mimic natural biochemicals in doses that create cravings when the substance is withdrawn. Part of this tendency may be our childlike resistance to authority figures telling us what is good and bad. Whatever the explanation, once a toxic habit is established, the ritual itself provides reinforcement for the behavior. For example, just the familiar act of pouring a drink or lighting up a cigarette may soothe anxiety. The problem, of course, is that the short-term relief provided by the behavior may predispose us to long-term suffering.

Our experience at the Chopra Center has taught us that in order for someone to release something that is not serving them well, several components must be in place. In order to unravel a toxic conditioned pattern and replace it with a nourishing one, you will need to systematically reinforce the transformation with your thoughts and choices. There are four critical steps to relinquishing something toxic in your life.

The Intention to Detoxify

The first important step is to *form a clear and strong intention.* If you are not convinced that your life will be better as a result of eliminating something toxic, you will not have the motivation or will to make the change. It is best to formulate your intention in a positive rather than a negative way. If you want to stop smoking, state your intention as "I want to breathe more easily and feel comfortable in my body without the need for tobacco," rather than "I need to get rid of these horrible cigarettes from my life." If your desire is to stop drinking alcohol, formulate the intention that you wish to feel safe and centered without the need for self-medication. If you want to lose weight, formulate the intention that you want a healthy, fit body. Create a clear vision of how your life will be better as a result of letting go of the toxin. If you are struggling with an addiction that you have the clear intention to release, try the "Envisioning Wholeness" process on the next page.

If you are habitually consuming a toxic substance that you know is not serving you well, make the commitment now to release it. Form a clear intention and reinforce your affirmations:

I commit to releasing ________ from my life,
once and forever.
Without ________ in my life,
I look and feel a healthy ____ years old.

Throughout the day, practice your affirmation and the envisioning of your life free from the toxic habit until your body/mind is spontaneously resonating with this vision for your life. Develop a clear vision of your new reality and create it through all your daily choices.

Envisioning Wholeness

Sit comfortably, close your eyes, and for several minutes quiet your inner dialogue through meditation. If you have not been instructed in Primordial Sound Meditation, practice the breathing awareness meditation as described in Chapter 3. Now, begin to envision your life free from the negative effects of the life-damaging habit. Imagine your home and work environment, unencumbered by the addiction. Picture how your body looks, smells, and feels free from the toxic effects of the dependency. Imagine the nourishing relationships with your friends and loved ones. Experience on the screen of your consciousness the vitality, comfort, and sense of competence you have, liberated from the negative pattern that is impacting your life. Allow this vision of wholeness to permeate every cell in your body.

Practice Mindfulness

The second step is to *turn the toxic behavior into a mindful meditation.* This means shifting into a mode of witnessing awareness while you are performing the action. If you want to eliminate smoking, focus your full attention on the action. Sit quietly and observe yourself as you slowly reach for your pack, remove a cigarette, light up, and inhale. Feel the sensations in your body and stop when your need has been fulfilled.

Very few people actually enjoy their first smoke or taste of whiskey, which reflects the inherent wisdom of the body. It is only after you have overridden your body's signals with false mental messages—"I look cool when I smoke."

"Drinking alcohol makes me grown-up." "Doing drugs is hip."—that your physiological impulses stop being sent. In its effort to conserve energy, if we do not heed our internal signals, the body stops sending them. Performing the habitual action with "beginner's awareness" will help you experience the honest effects of the substance.

Systemically Detoxify

The third step is to *start a general detoxification program*. Set a stop date and use the opportunity to clear both your mind and body. Focusing on purification will help shorten the period of withdrawal discomfort and help your mind and body shift into a healthier mode of functioning. Drink lots of fresh fruit and vegetable juices during this time. Try fruit juices in the morning, mixed fruit and vegetable juices during the day, and vegetable juices and blended vegetable soups in the evening. We often recommend gingerroot tea, prepared by adding one teaspoon of freshly grated root to a pint of hot water. Simplify your diet for a few days, favoring whole grains, steamed vegetables, and lentil soups. Take hot baths or go to a sauna or steam room to encourage the removal of toxins through your skin.

Spend at least some time every day walking in a park or along a stream, lake, or ocean. Inhale fresh air, feel the sun on your face, and wiggle your feet in the sand or grass. Directly connect with nature's purifying influence.

This is a good time to start a healthy daily routine. Commit to meditating twice a day, getting to bed before 10:30 P.M. and rising at sunrise. Drink plenty of water. Begin a regular exercise program. Get some body work to help mobilize the toxins from your body. Start a healthy diet. The more positive things you introduce into your life, the easier it will be to eliminate whatever is toxic.

Panchakarma

Ayurveda recommends a total detoxification program known as Panchakarma, which means the purifying actions. The full program as offered at the Chopra Center prescribes a systematic process to identify, mobilize, and eliminate stored toxins in the body. Luxurious oil massages are followed by heat treatments and then some type of eliminative procedure to discharge toxins through the digestive tract or nasal passages.

You can perform a gentle detoxification program at home by following these steps:

1. Follow a simplified diet for five days with plenty of steamed vegetables, grains, and lentil soup. Eliminate fried foods, fermented foods, dairy, animal products, and refined carbohydrates during this time.
2. For three days eat sesame seeds and golden raisins to lubricate your digestive tract. Prepare a one-to-one mix of ⅛ cup of white sesame seeds and ⅛ cup of golden raisins. Ingest a teaspoon of the mixture one hour before or two hours after each meal. If you have any trouble digesting seeds, take ½ teaspoon of sesame oil with three to four raisins three times a day.
3. Drink plenty of gingerroot tea by grating one teaspoon of fresh gingerroot per pint of hot water and sipping it throughout the day. It is easiest if you get a thermos bottle so you can keep the tea with you. Try drinking at least one liter per day.
4. On the evening of the fourth day, perform an oil massage (see pages 74–76) and soak in a hot bath.
5. Around ten P.M., take a teaspoon of yogurt with a dose of standardized senna extract. We recommend Senokot. Most people will get a good elimination with four tablets before bedtime. Expect a few loose bowel

movements within the next six to eight hours.

6. Eat lightly the next day, gradually reintroducing more complex foods into your diet.

Rejuvenation

The final step is to *fill the space* previously occupied by the noxious substance with something nourishing. We find the most important "thing" to fill the emptiness is the peace, comfort, and awareness that come from meditation. When people who have been indulging a life-damaging habit begin meditating, they often spontaneously lose their desire for the toxic experience. When someone who has relinquished a toxic habit complains that they have started it up again, the first question we ask is "Are you still meditating?" Invariably the answer is no, often because their life was becoming so dynamic, their meditation time became a lower priority. Regularly accessing the quiet, expanded state of awareness through meditation is an essential component of releasing noxious habits.

Other approaches that can be useful in filling the space left by the habitual behavior include starting an exercise program, taking classes in a subject that is fascinating to you, and dedicating yourself to healing your relationships. It is sad how often a toxic behavior that compensates for a lack of love actually reduces the likelihood of finding genuine love. It can be very helpful to join support groups of people who have gone or are going through the transformation you are seeking. Associate with people who support your healthy choices and minimize your exposure to those looking to reinforce their toxic habits by disparaging your efforts to change your life.

The elimination of toxins awakens
the capacity for renewal.

Water—Nature's Purifier

A very simple but powerful purification technique is to boost your intake of water. The human body is approximately three-fourths water and most biochemical reactions operate best within a narrow window of concentration. Several scientific studies have found that our sensitivity to thirst diminishes as we age, so we become at risk for developing subtle levels of dehydration of which we may not be consciously aware. Most people do not drink enough water, which can lead to a host of symptoms. Headaches, constipation, dry skin, fatigue, and indigestion may actually reflect subtle dehydration.

Some physicians have gone as far as to suggest that many common health concerns, including high blood pressure, asthma, and chronic pain have their origins in dehydration.

Assuming that you do not have kidney or liver problems, we recommend getting into the habit of drinking water throughout the day. You can calculate the recommended number of ounces of daily water intake by dividing your weight in pounds by two.

____________________	÷ 2 =	______________
Your weight in pounds		Target heart rate

For example, if you weigh 160 pounds, your daily water intake should be 80 ounces or 10 cups per day. Most bottled water comes in half-liter containers, equivalent to just over two cups, so this would mean drinking five bottles per day. Soda beverages, tea, and coffee do not count, as their caffeine content has a diuretic effect. Similarly, alcohol also causes water loss and does not contribute to rehydration. If you are active in sports, taking diuretics, or live in a hot, dry climate, increase your daily intake by another 10 to 15 percent. Favor water-rich fruits and vegetables including cantaloupe, grapefruit, peaches, watermelon, asparagus, peppers, carrots, and mushrooms. Minimize your intake of artificially sweetened beverages. When you are drinking enough water you will feel the need to empty your bladder about every two hours.

Many people who follow this water routine report that they more easily lose unwanted weight and have more energy and less chronic aches and pains. Drinking plenty of fresh, pure water is one of the simplest and least expensive ways to reverse the aging process.

Eliminate Toxic Foods

Freshly grown and lovingly prepared foods are richest in Prana, or life energy. Foods that have been sitting around for months in a can on your shelf are less likely to nourish your body, mind, and spirit. Start a vegetable garden in your backyard and grow fresh herbs and spices to enhance your meals. Shop at your local farmer's markets and take the time to prepare delicious meals, applying the principles explored in Chapter 3. If you find yourself regularly eating frozen, canned, microwaved, or highly processed foods, shift your time priorities to make nourishing yourself higher on your list. Make the preparation of meals a family or community experience so you can enjoy the process as well as the product.

There is increasing evidence that the pesticides and artificial fertilizers used in modern agriculture are taking their toll on our health. These synthetic chemicals are finding their way into our air and water supply. They have been implicated as possibly contributing to a number of different cancers, particularly of the reproductive system.

Studies have shown that it takes diligent washing to remove the pesticide residues that are present on fruits and vegetables. For these reasons, we encourage you to favor organically grown foods. Although they cost more, you can feel confident that you and your family are not consuming unnecessary toxins along with your meals. You will also know that you are doing your share to reduce the accumulation of toxins in your environment.

Release Toxic Emotions

Although we are all aware of the health-depleting effects of toxic substances and toxic foods, toxic emotions are often the most harmful accelerators of the aging process. Whenever you carry resentment, hostility, regret, or grievances in your heart, your vitality is eroded. Try this simple practice:

- Find a quiet place, sit comfortably, and close your eyes.

- Now take a few minutes to settle your mind with the So Hum meditation.
- After a little while, bring your attention into your body and scan it for any area of tension or resistance. If you identify a place of congestion, have the intention to let it go.
- Bring your attention into your heart and acknowledge all the things for which you feel grateful.
- Now listen to your heart and ask yourself the question, "What am I carrying with me from the past that is no longer serving me well in the present?"
- If you identify any encumbrances in your heart, have the intention to release them now. Let go of any resentments, grievances, or regrets that you find.
- As you release these toxic emotions, see if you can find the gift that this toxic emotion was hiding. For example, if you felt pain as a result of someone's behavior, the gift may be that you learned more self-reliance.
- Make the commitment to regularly acknowledge gratitude and relinquish all grievances from your heart.

Encumbering your heart with toxic emotions prevents you from fully experiencing the magic, mystery, and joy that is available to you right now. Make the commitment to release the resentments, regrets, and grievances that are causing more harm to you than anyone else.

The process of releasing emotional toxins is similar to that for releasing physical ones. You must first have a clear intention that you want to replace life-depleting emotions with life-enhancing ones. The metabolism of regret and resentment into compassion and forgiveness can dramatically awaken your body, mind, and spirit to your primordial vital energy.

Write about the history that created the toxic emotion, describing both what happened and how you feel as a result of the situation. Studies have shown that journaling about upsetting emotional experiences can improve your immune function, as well as help you gain clarity and insight. In his book *Nonviolent Communication,* psychologist Marshall Rosenberg teaches an emotional vocabulary that avoids victimization. Steer clear from words like abandoned, abused, neglected, and mistreated; instead, describe the actual feelings of anger, sadness, loneliness, and fear that the circumstance evoked.

Once you have written about the circumstances leading to the toxic emotions, perform some physical ritual with the intention of releasing the hold these feelings have on your soul. Do some deep breathing, get a massage, pound a pillow, dance with abandon, or go for a long run until your body has released the tension that is stored with the emotion. Then, open your heart to feelings that generate the age-reversing emotions of forgiveness, harmony, laughter, and love rather than the entropy evoking ones of anguish, resentment, regret, and despair.

Toxic emotions are often the most harmful accelerators of the aging process. Commit to releasing them from your heart and mind.

Transform or Release Toxic Relationships

You may, at times, find yourself in relationships that are laced with conflict. Although you may enjoy the passion and drama these relationships generate, over time, they will inevitably make you feel older and depleted. It is essential that you transform toxic relationships into nourishing ones. If you accept that reality is a selective act of perception and interpretation, the most empowering way to transform a relationship is to change the way you view the other person.

Every relationship is a mirror that can show

you some aspect of yourself. When you are engaged in conflict, ask yourself, "What is this situation telling me about my own nature?" Try this simple exercise that can be helpful in revealing the hidden meaning in a difficult relationship.

Write down as many traits as you can think of that describe the person with whom you are having problems.

____________________ ____________________

____________________ ____________________

____________________ ____________________

Now look again at each descriptive word and see which ones create an emotional charge in you. For example, you may have described your manager as:

Controlling *Argumentative*
Needy *Uncompromising*
Unappreciative *Stubborn*

As you review your list, you may see traits that *really* irritate you: controlling, needy, unappreciative, and stubborn. Now look at yourself. Are these words that others might use to describe you? Do you have the tendency to reflect these traits? Have you expressed these qualities in the past? More often than not, the traits that bother you the most in another person are the ones you try hardest to deny in yourself. As you embrace these darker qualities in your own heart, you may find yourself less inclined to judge someone else for expressing them. As you relinquish your judgment and interpretation, you may open to the possibility that there are other qualities that may be attractive in the person, which you have not allowed yourself to see.

Meeting Your Needs

Relationships thrive when both parties feel their needs are being met and struggle when they are not. Put very simply: You feel good when your needs are being met and bad when they are not. Not getting your needs met leads to stress, toxic emotions, and toxic relationships. Learning to express your needs and emotions in a healthy way fosters nourishing relationships and reverses aging.

As infants, we expect our caregivers to fulfill our needs, even if we don't know what they are. We wail a few times and anticipate Mother scrambling to determine if we are hungry, cold, tired, bored, or just want to be held. We carry these same desires into adulthood and become hurt, frustrated, angry, or depressed when our lovers, friends, or associates are unable to immediately figure out what we need and give it to us. This is not an approach that is likely to be successful. Let's explore a more effective way to express your needs and emotions.

The Dialogue of Needs

The humanistic psychologist Abraham Maslow described five basic needs that drive us all. First, we have basic physiological needs, such as food, water, and protection against extreme heat or cold. Once these needs are met we are motivated by the need for safety and security. We all want to feel protected from physical and emotional harm. The third need is social—the need for community, friendship, love, and belonging. As these needs are met we have the need for self-esteem. At this level, achievement, respect, recognition, and status are sought. The final need is to find meaning, beauty, and wisdom in life. Maslow called this final step self-actualization. In Eastern traditions this is the state of enlightenment.

Self-actualized people are accepting, spontaneous, natural, and simple. They are dedicated to a life of meaning and creativity. They are as comfortable alone as they are in intimate personal relationships. They are playful and laugh easily. They know how to meet their needs.

In his book *Nonviolent Communication,* Marshall Rosenberg describes a simple process to enhance the chances of getting your needs met. Whenever your needs are not met and you become upset, first ask yourself, "What am I observing?" Rather than saying to the other person "You are always late to every date," say "We agreed to meet at noon and you did not arrive until 12:30 P.M." Separate your judgments and evaluation from your observations and you will be less likely to trigger defensiveness.

The second step is to identify what you are feeling. Develop a rich emotional vocabulary that does not make you a victim. Avoid words that require someone else to be there for you to experience your emotions, such as ignored, rejected, neglected, abandoned, or abused. You are empowered when you say you feel alarmed, annoyed, exhausted, frightened, lonely, outraged, or sad, but you give away your power when you use the vocabulary of the victim.

The third step is to determine what you actually need from the situation. If you cannot be clear on what your needs are, it's very unlikely that the other person is in a better position to figure it out.

The fourth step is to formulate a specific request. Ask for what you need as specifically as possible. Rather than demanding "You need to spend more time with me or else!," rephrase it in the form of a request: "Are you willing to come home an hour early from work Wednesday afternoon so we can take a walk together?" People are much more likely to respond to a request than a demand.

We would add a fifth step to Dr. Rosenberg's original four. Whether your request is met or not, ask yourself, what is the gift in this situation? What can you learn from this circumstance about yourself and life? What is the lesson that can raise you to a higher level of awareness? Find the gift, even if it is not the one you originally anticipated.

Make the commitment to communicate your needs consciously, and you will waste a lot less energy in conflict. Accept your differences as a cause of celebration, rather than finding it necessary to make the other person wrong. Because we believe that cultivating loving relationships is such an important component of reversing the aging process, we devote an entire step to it in Chapter 10.

Accept your differences as a cause of celebration.

Release Toxic Work

Most people spend a good portion of their life on the job. So ideally work should afford the opportunity to express your creativity, to interact meaningfully with your coworkers, and to provide the material security you seek. Unfortunately, many people find their workplace to be a source of stress rather than fulfillment, and consequently, aging is accelerated rather than reversed.

The world would be a better place if we all could do what made us happy, while expressing our unique talents in service to others and ourselves. According to Ayurveda, this is the state of living in *dharma,* or fulfilling your purpose in life. Even if you are not able to earn a living doing exactly what you like doing best, see if you can bring some aliveness to your workplace.

- Try connecting more openly with your coworkers so your work environment is emotionally healthier.
- Observe your environment and see if you can improve the sounds, sights, or smells that surround you.
- Look for opportunities to align your work with your values, needs, and beliefs.

Life is precious and you have the right to perform work that is meaningful. A test to see if you are in your dharma is to notice how often you look at the time. If your inner dialogue tells you that time is creeping by very slowly and you cannot wait to get off work, you are probably not in a position that is fully expressing your purpose in life. If, on the other hand, you find that time flies while you are engaged, it is a good clue that this work is the type that can help you grow younger. Listen to the signals that your body and mind are communicating and commit to spending your day creating greater fulfillment for you and those in your life.

Reversing the Appearance of Aging

The field of energy, information, and intelligence commonly known as the skin is your largest and most adaptable organ. As the boundary zone between your inner and outer worlds, the skin protects your tissues, cells, and molecules from the onslaught of microorganisms, temperature extremes, ultraviolet and infrared radiation, and chemical pollutants present in your environment. It constantly monitors stimuli from your surroundings through its innumerable touch, temperature, and pain receptors, and sends this information to your brain on a moment-to-moment basis. Your soft pliant skin has the remarkable ability to differentiate itself into the long strands of your hair or your flat hard nails by rearranging its collagen molecules. It is the site of vitamin D activation, crucial for maintaining strong bones. The skin contains sweat glands, oil glands, fat cells, nerve fibers, immune cells, and miles of blood vessels and is essential in your regulation of body temperature and hydration. The skin is literally your face to the world.

Following a few basic skin care principles can reverse the appearance of aging. There are three important steps you must take as part of an age-reversing skin care program: (1) purify, (2) revitalize, and (3) replenish.

Purify

Your skin reflects the purity of your entire body. The principles of a healthy diet, nutritional supplementation, and detoxification will pay their rewards in the quality of your skin. In addition to generally healthy lifestyle choices, you must carefully clean your skin once or twice daily to remove local toxins that block your skin pores and predispose you to infections.

It is generally best to avoid soaps that contain

harsh detergents and to use natural cleansers. Ayurveda recommends the use of herbal cleansing powders that remove toxins and excessive oils while reestablishing acid-base balance. An easily mixed formula that you can make at home includes equal parts dried chickpea flour, dry milk powder, nutmeg, lemon peel, and ground coriander. Use about half a teaspoon with water to make a paste and gently apply it to your moistened face. As it begins to dry, rinse off the powder.

If you wish to experiment with traditional Ayurvedic cleansing herbs, try adding neem, manjistha, or sandalwood powder. A basic principle regarding the cleansing product is not to use anything on your skin that you wouldn't be comfortable putting into your stomach.

Moist herbalized steam treatments are also helpful in opening clogged pores and releasing toxins. Once a week, treat yourself to a facial steam bath to which you add a few drops of essential oil. Lavender, juniper, rosemary, bergamot, or sage all have purifying effects on the body.

Revitalize

The second step to reverse the appearance of aging is skin revitalization. Stimulating the collagen fibers that support the skin can improve its tone and appearance. Many modern skin care products contain natural acids that stimulate the cells that produce collagen, such as glycolic acid, azelaic acid, and lactic acid. Skin care products with these acids in higher concentration will cause some peeling and should be used under the supervision of a skilled skin care specialist. Milder revitalizing treatments can be applied at home using readily available natural products.

Yogurt, lemon juice, and grapefruit juice can have a mild stimulating effect. Fresh yogurt can be applied directly to your skin and left on for five minutes before rinsing. Dilute lemon juice or grapefruit juice with an equal part of aloe vera juice and apply to the skin. Leave on for two minutes and then rinse. If your skin is oily, you can do this every day. If your skin tends to be dry or reactive, dilute the solution further and use every second or third day.

Replenish

After cleansing and revitalizing, the skin needs to be replenished. Use a pure vegetable or nut oil to which a few drops of an essential flower or herb oil has been added. Try mixing almond, jojoba, avocado, or sunflower oil with rose, lavender, sandalwood, jasmine, geranium, or lemon essential oils. Apply a small amount and allow it to be absorbed naturally. Use more if your skin is on the dry side. Source books on natural beauty care are listed in the references for this chapter.

Sun Protection

Always use sunscreen when you are outdoors. Ultraviolet radiation leads to collagen damage, wrinkling, and skin cancer. Prevention is much better than cure, so be aware of the potentially damaging effects of sun on your skin. This is particularly important if you live in a hot climate or at higher altitudes. Teach your children to use sunscreen to prevent unnecessary skin problems later in their lives.

Every day in every way,
I am increasing my mental and physical capacity.
My Biostat is set at a healthy ____ years of age.
I look and feel a healthy ____ years old.

I am reversing my biological age:

- *By changing my perception of my body, its aging and time;*

- *Through two kinds of deep rest—restful awareness and restful sleep;*
- *By nurturing my body through healthy foods;*
- *By using nutritional complements wisely;*
- *By enhancing mind/body integration;*
- *Through exercise; and*
- *By eliminating toxins from my life.*

9

You Can Reverse Your Biological Age by Cultivating Flexibility and Creativity in Consciousness

ACTION STEP #8

I am reversing my biological age by cultivating flexibility and creativity in my consciousness.
I put flexibility into practice by:

1. *Learning to let go when things don't seem to go my way.*
2. *Practicing the wisdom of uncertainty—not being attached to outcome and letting go of the need to control.*
3. *Learning to forgive by relinquishing grievances, resentments, and regrets.*

I put creativity into practice by:

1. *Learning the nine-step creative response.*
2. *Applying the creative response to all the challenges and/or problems in my life.*
3. *Helping others to solve their problems by teaching them the creative response.*

Aging is associated with rigidit and decay.
Youth is associated with flexibility
and creativity.
Both flexibility and creativity
are learned behaviors.
By cultivating flexibility and creativity
in consciousness,you renew yourself
in every moment and
reverse the aging process.
An ancient Vedic aphorism says,
"Infinite flexibility and creativity
are the secrets to immortality."

You can reverse your biological age by cultivating flexibility and creativity in consciousness. When we consider growing older we usually think of becoming less flexible and creative. Our language of aging reflects this view. We use expressions like "You can't teach an old dog new tricks," or "I'm too old to change," or "He's just too set in his ways." In both modern and Vedic sciences, the loss of flexibility and creativity is a result of increasing inertia, entropy, and disorder in the body/mind system.

According to Vedic theory there are three fundamental forces at work in the universe: *Sattwa, Rajas,* and *Tamas.* Sattwa is the force of creativity, evolution, and transformation. Tamas is the force of stability, resistance, and inertia. Rajas is the tension between the forces of creativity and inertia. As children and adolescents we are dominated by change, flexibility, and creativity and have a preponderance of natural Sattwa. Our brains and our behavior reflect our tremendous capability to expand, adapt, transform, and evolve and our willingness and desire to experience and learn new things. As adults we see the rise of Rajas. This is a result of the everyday stresses of life and our attachment to outcomes, as we seek to prove ourselves in the world. As we age we become increasingly concerned about security and stability and Tamas begins to predominate. This stability is reflected in our behaviors and in the connections between the neurons in our brains. Stability leads to stagnation, stagnation leads to decay, decay leads to disorder and entropy, and ultimately to death.

Death is the soul's response to the loss of flexibility. When your physiology has lost the flexibility and creativity to further integrate the energy and information of your life experiences, the soul goes into incubation. According to Vedic wisdom, when the soul needs to digest the experiences of a lifetime, it first incubates and then takes a quantum leap into a new context and a new body/mind. In Eastern wisdom traditions this is the process of reincarnation—incarnating into a new life experience.

Rather than waiting for death to take a quantum leap into a new life experience, why not take the quantum leap while you are alive? This way you can incarnate (literally reincarnate) on an ongoing basis. This requires learning two basic and fundamental behavior patterns:

(1) *flexibility,* which comes from letting go, and (2) *creativity,* which involves intention, incubation, and incarnation. By learning to incorporate flexibility and creativity as your evolving behavioral pattern, you will master on a daily basis what most people have to literally die for—to incarnate and create a new body/mind. Let's explore these two qualities that are the foundation of eternal youth.

By cultivating flexibility and creativity in consciousness, you renew yourself in every moment and reverse the aging process.

Flexibility

The essence of flexibility is the willingness to let go. Surveys of centenarians (people who have lived at least one hundred years) often ask, "What do you believe are the reasons that account for your long and healthy life? Is it your diet? Have you been exercising your whole life? Have you avoided tobacco? Do you drink alcohol?" The intent of these questions, of course, is to identify common principles that could help us all live longer, healthier lives. Surprisingly, none of these questions clearly reveals the secret to longevity. The most common explanation that our most senior citizens offer for their long life is *their ability to let go.*

Long-living people have flexibility and resiliency when facing the inevitable challenges in life. If you live to be a hundred years old, chances are good you have experienced challenges and losses, yet these super seniors have been able to move through adversity and get on with their lives. They relinquish their hold on experiences that do not serve them. They let go and move on.

From an Ayurvedic perspective, this ability to deal with what is happening but not incur residual damage is a symptom of strong digestive power, known in Sanskrit as *Agni.* The expression "digestive power" is applied not just to the ability to digest foods but to digest all experiences in life. Agni is the root of the English word ignite, referring to the power of fire to metabolize things. When your digestive force is powerful, you are capable of extracting the nourishment you need from any experience and eliminating whatever is not serving you. A strong Agni enables you to digest what life presents without carrying unprocessed residues, which inhibit your ability to fully embrace life. A strong digestive power is an essential feature of people who live long, vital lives.

Learning to let go is necessary because life is a

process of continual change and transformation. Attempting to stop change by holding on is fighting the natural force of evolution. Ultimately, nature will have its way, and your struggle against the river of life will exact its toll on your physiology. The wear and tear born of resistance accelerates aging. Relinquishing your resistance and embracing change reverses aging.

Learning to let go does not mean relinquishing your intentions. Your intentions and desires orchestrate the course of your life and catalyze the experiences you need to evolve to higher levels of awareness. Flexibility does not require letting go of intentions. Flexibility does, however, require letting go of your attachment to a specific outcome. You cannot control the outcome of a situation, and holding rigidly to your idea about how things should be leads to strain, stress, and aging. Whenever it appears that your intended outcome is not the one manifesting, bear in mind the following expression, which we heard from a spiritual teacher:

> *When things don't seem to go my way, I let go of my attachment to how I think they should be, trusting that I am not seeing the big picture. If I knew the big picture I would understand that there is a reason for things unfolding the way they*

are, and that the cosmos has a plan for me much grander than anything I have conceived.

Letting go and detaching from outcome is the essence of genuine power and offers the only real possibility of security. Detachment from a particular outcome derives from trust in the intelligence of the universe and your connection to it. It implies a willingness to step into the unknown—the field of all possibilities. This is the real meaning of flexibility. Attachment to the known is attachment to the past. The past is stability. The past is inertia. The past is entropy. The past is stagnation. Attachment to the known—attachment to the past—accelerates aging.

Most people spend their entire lives seeking security through their attachments. Attachments are usually to positions and possessions. Because these attachments rarely bring security or happiness, people often believe their problem is that they need greater positions or more possessions. The internal conversation sounds like this: "If I just had more money . . . if I just had a better job . . . if I just had a more passionate relationship . . . then I would feel secure and happy." Money, positions, possession, and titles are symbols of security. Symbols of security cannot substitute for real security, which can only come from within.

Paradoxically, finding genuine and lasting security comes from surrendering to the wisdom of uncertainty. It means cultivating an inner attitude of curiosity and acceptance. It means detaching from a particular outcome and developing the mind-set that whatever occurs is the most evolutionary outcome at the time. This state of flexibility, in which you are able to embrace the unknown and detach from a particular outcome, reverses the aging process.

Relinquishing your resistance and embracing change reverses aging.

Present-Moment Awareness

The Buddhists have an expression: "Nothing should be clung to as me or mine." Nothing you identify with can really be called yours. Although you may consider the physical vehicle you inhabit as your body, you know by now that every atom comprising it is only on temporary loan from your environment. Within a year, almost every atom that you currently call yours will no longer be within the boundaries of your skin. Your thoughts are not really your thoughts. They are part of the collective mind. A hundred years ago, you could not have had the thought "I am flying on a 747 jet to Las Vegas," because these concepts were not yet a part of the collective mind. Your emotions are not your emotions. Every emotion you have ever had—elation, despair, joy, frustration, ecstasy, jealousy—has been experienced by people since the beginning of humanity. Not a single molecule, not a single thought, not a single emotion you have ever had is uniquely yours. You are part of a larger scheme. You are woven from a few strands in the infinite cosmic web of energy, transformation, and intelligence.

"Nothing should be clung to as me or mine." Underlying this prescription is the recognition that all stress in life results from either grasping or aversion. When you hold on to anything, be it a material object, a position, or a relationship, you constrict your awareness and accelerate aging. You accelerate aging because, at a subtle level, every attachment is accompanied by fear—fear of loss, fear of losing control, fear of losing approval. When you evoke fear you set into motion the physiology of stress that accelerates biological aging. You must let go of this fear in order to reverse aging.

The inclination of the mind is to lean toward something that you hope will bring pleasure or away from something that you fear will bring pain. As a result of this tendency, of this inclination, you are unable to remain in the present moment.

When you find yourself out of the present moment, ask yourself, "What is wrong with this moment?" You will see that there are only two possibilities: either you are resisting it or you are just not in it. If you are resisting it, consciously surrender to the here and now. If you are just not in it, gently bring yourself back to the present. Open yourself to the infinite possibilities that the present moment offers.

You can cultivate present-moment awareness through the practice of alert witnessing—shifting your attention from that which is observed to the silent ever-present witness to the observation. In the midst of observation, come back to the self.

Your observations change on a moment-to-moment basis. If you identify who you are with your observations, your identity has no permanence. It becomes a moment-to-moment fabrication. When you identify yourself with the objects of your perception, which are in constant flux, you sacrifice your true self for the objects of your self-image. If you identify yourself as the president of a company, as the owner of a luxury car, as the manager of an artist or musician, your sense of self is dependent upon an external source. This is sometimes known as agency power because your power derives from attachment to an external agency, be it an organization, bank account, or relationship. The problem with agency power is that when the attachment ends, so does the power and your sense of self.

The opposite of agency power is self-power, which comes from your inner connection to Spirit. Underlying all your observations and experiences in life, underlying all your attachments to people, situations, and circumstances, is a domain of ever-present witnessing awareness. This is your true self; this is your Spirit.

In alert witnessing you shift your attention from goal orientation to process orientation. You become completely flexible. You are unattached to outcome. You are comfortable in the realm of uncertainty. When Spirit is your internal reference point you neither anticipate nor resist—you simply allow. When you walk a certain road, you have the intention to reach a particular destination, but if more interesting opportunities present themselves along the way, then have the flexible inner attitude to go with the flow. This process can be summed up in one statement, "Take it as it comes." The process becomes the goal.

Whenever you find yourself grasping or recoiling, anticipating or resisting, shift your attention to your witnessing self. In this simple process of coming back to the self, you return to the present moment. The present moment is the doorway to the field of infinite possibilities. The present moment is characterized by infinite flexibility. Living in present-moment awareness reverses the aging process.

When you evoke fear you set into motion the physiology of stress that accelerates biological aging. You must let go of this fear in order to reverse aging.

Forgiveness

The great Vedic scholar Eknath Easwawan tells a poignant story. At the end of a lifetime, a person's soul goes to a plane of existence where each life is reviewed. The soul enters a theater in which a movie of the recent life is playing. The soul begins watching the movie but often has to turn away because of terribly uncomfortable scenes. Sins of omission and sins of commission cramp the heart, and the scene becomes too painful to watch. As a result of not being able to watch the complete movie, important life lessons are missed, and the soul must reincarnate to learn them in the next lifetime.

According to this story, the primary cause for not being able to watch the painful scenes of life is a lack of forgiveness—for others and for oneself. Forgiveness is the essence of letting go. It means relinquishing attachments to the past and clearing encumbrances that constrict the heart. These constrictions are the source of inertia, entropy, and aging. Release them to grow younger. Try this simple exercise:

Close your eyes, bring your attention into your heart and ask if you are holding on to any grievances, hostilities, resentments, or regrets. If any come to mind, ask what occurred that led to the blockage in your heart. Then, ask what needs to occur now in order to release these toxins. Look for the gift that every life experience offers, even painful ones, and express your gratitude for the experience.

Remember this beautiful expression from *A Course in Miracles* and refer to it often: "Every decision I make is a choice between a grievance and a miracle."

We encourage you to choose a miracle. When things do not go the way you think they should, you could indulge in self-pity. You could complain and gripe that life isn't fair. You could lament about what you are not getting and make yourself and everyone around you miserable. Or you could see the situation as another opportunity for surrender, flexibility, and expansion. Grievances, hostilities, resentments, and regrets become festering emotional wounds that accelerate aging. Forgive and forget and you will reverse the aging process.

Breaking Habitual Patterns

It's easy to become trapped in habitual patterns that do not serve you well and promote inflexibility. Therefore it is very helpful to consciously cultivate flexibility by relinquishing things in your life and creating new patterns of thinking and behaving. Practicing flexibility creates flexibility in your nervous system by challenging your brain cells to make new associations. The neurons in your nervous system and the choices in your life are engaged in a continuous feedback loop. In your willingness to try new things, your neural networks become more flexible and open to new perceptions, interpretations, and choices, which in turn support new interneuronal connections.

Here are a few suggestions of things you can do to break out of your habitual behavioral patterns. Try them for a week and observe what happens to your body and mind.

- Change your diet
- Change your exercise program
- Change your route to work

- Change your bedtime
- Meditate longer
- Buy different clothing
- Wear new colors
- Listen to different kinds of music
- Stop wearing a watch
- Wear your watch on the other wrist
- Go out to lunch with someone new
- Try a new restaurant
- Change your opinion about something or someone
- Call a friend you haven't spoken to in years
- Answer the phone differently
- Change your voice mail message
- Read a book that you usually wouldn't consider
- Watch a different television show
- Listen to a different radio station
- Take a new class

Let go of old ways and you will feel renewed. Learning to be flexible means learning to access the most flexible domain of your being—the field of timeless awareness underlying your mind and body. This realm of flexibility is the basis of growing younger. Immerse yourself in this field of infinite flexibility on a daily basis through meditation. Have the conscious intention to think and act flexibly. Practice letting go whenever holding on is no longer serving you.

Creativity

Once you have cultivated flexibility you are ready for creativity. Without flexibility there can be no creativity. According to Amit Goswami, author of *Quantum Creativity,* creativity is a discontinuous, nonalgorithmic quantum jump from one pattern of thinking into a completely new one. It is a quantum leap—a paradigm shift—from one pattern to another without progressing through incremental steps in between. All the great creative advances in the worlds of art, music, architecture, or science represent new leaps of imagination that could not have been predicted on the basis of the prevailing patterns. Once the creative leap is made, be it Einstein's theory of relativity, Picasso's cubism, or music by the Beatles, the world is forever changed.

You are by nature a creative being, although you may no longer think of yourself this way. As a child you had a rich imagination, which is the source of all creativity. Your youthful flexibility and present-moment awareness allowed for new perceptions and interpretations on an ongoing basis. You were capable of creating entire worlds with your imagination, whether it was building sand castles at the beach or playing with your make-believe family of dolls. Today, the very fact that you are alive is evidence of your creativity, for you are co-creating your reality every moment. You are creating a new body/mind with every impulse of experience and every breath you take. Learn to reawaken your creative response and you will recapture the energy and enthusiasm of youth. In addition to helping you grow younger, the creative process can be applied to healing, relationships, the arts, and business.

Taking a Creative Leap

Creativity is the process of taking the raw energy, information, and material of the universe and transforming it into something that has never been created before. Whether you are creating an original work of art, a new piece of music, a unique software program, or a healing response to an illness, creativity requires a leap in awareness. If you are improving on something that already exists, that is innovation. Creativity brings something into existence that has never been here before.

There are nine basic steps to the creative

response. Become conscious of these steps and use the creative response whenever you are facing an issue or challenge in your life. You have unlimited creative potential that can be used to solve any problem you are facing.

Intended Outcome

The first step of the creative response is to have a clear *intended outcome.* You must have a clear vision of what it is that you want to have unfold. If you are not certain about what you want, you are unlikely to fulfill your needs. State your intended outcome in clear positive language: "I have a healthy body with abundant energy." "My intimate relationships are loving and nurturing." Avoid defining your intentions in terms of what you don't want. Rather than saying "I want to leave this dreadful job," state your intention as "I have a position that enables me to express my full potential."

Write down your intentions and review them regularly to be certain that they reflect your current desires. Although living in a state of flexibility implies not being attached to a particular outcome, it is still essential that you have unambiguous intentions. Formulate a clear intention and be detached from the outcome.

Information Gathering

The second step is *information gathering.* In this stage, learn everything that is available about the issue you are facing. Become an expert on the challenge that confronts you, recognizing that your particular variation is unique. Read books, do research, use the Internet, explore spiritual literature, go to lectures, participate in workshops, speak with friends and family. Gather information from every possible source without judging or filtering. Pay attention to the sensations in your body as you learn what others have to say about your issue, noting which approaches feel comfortable for you and which feel uncomfortable.

Information Reshuffling and Information Analysis

As you gather information, your mind will digest what you are learning, formatting the information in ways that are useful to you. This process of *information reshuffling* takes place on both conscious and subconscious levels. The data is analyzed looking for patterns that can provide clues to a new understanding of the issue.

Incubation

The fourth step is *incubation.* In incubation, you allow your awareness to settle into a more expanded state of consciousness through meditation. Incubation is the stage of surrender. Having formed your intention, gathered and reshuffled the information you obtained, the next step is to go beyond the rational mind and access a deeper domain of awareness to orchestrate the fulfillment of your intention. Use the So Hum meditation technique described in Chapter 3 to quiet and expand your mind. Review your intention for a few moments before you begin meditation and then let go. Letting go allows for something entirely new to arise in your awareness—something that you had not conceived of before.

Insight

When the conditions are right, you will experience the fifth step, which is *insight.* Insight results from the rearranging of the previous relationships and meanings into an entirely new context, which then allows for an entirely new interpretation. Insight is the creative leap—your perception and interpretation of the issue completely shifts. This new inner vision is the essence of the creative response. It precipitates from a domain of awareness that is nonlocal. The process of meditation allows you to enter into this nonlocal domain that exists for eternity in the gaps between your thoughts. When you are able to go beyond your ideas about how things should be, gaining access to this deeper domain, something unprecedented emerges. This is insight.

Inspiration

When the insight occurs, it spontaneously generates *inspiration.* The level of enthusiasm that wells up when insight dawns is a good barometer that the insight is a real creative leap. When you really see things in a new light, your entire mind/body becomes energized. You know in your mind that your insight is true and you feel in your body that the insight is right. Passion, exhilaration, excitement, joy, and enthusiasm are all signs that the insight that arose while you were incubating will solve your problem and fulfill your intention.

Implementation, Integration, Incarnation

It is now your task to translate the insight into action. Now that you know what is necessary to fulfill your intention, do it. Make the change, take the step, and *implement* the action to actualize the creative response. *Integrate* the change into your life. As you integrate and implement the insight into your thinking and behavior, you *incarnate* it in your body. It becomes a part of you, and as a result you are a new person. You have taken a creative leap and have become a new body/mind.

Archimedes, the Archetypal Creative Response

Archimedes was the greatest mathematician of his time. A third-century B.C. native of Syracuse, Sicily, he was asked by King Hiero to determine if the crown that was made for him was of pure gold *(Intention)*. Archimedes knew that if he could calculate the density of the crown he would be able to determine if any other metals had been added *(Information gathering)*. He knew that density was weight (mass) divided by volume. He could weigh the crown on a scale, but due to its irregular shape, he did not know how to find its precise volume. After considering this problem continuously for days *(Information reshuffling)*, he was convinced by his servant to let the puzzle go for a little while and take a warm bath *(Incubation)*. As he was lowering himself into the tub, he noticed that his body displaced an amount of water equal to his volume. This led to the idea *(Insight)* that he could calculate the density of the crown by determining how much water it displaced. He was so exuberant about his discovery *(Inspiration)* that legend has it he ran through the streets of Syracuse shouting "Eureka!," which in Greek means "I've found it!" As it turned out, the metalsmith had diluted the gold with silver.

As an example of how this might work on a personal level, consider a woman who is in constant turmoil because her spouse is not meeting her expectations. In her mind, he spends too much time alone or on the phone with friends and colleagues. As a result of her distress and anxiety she has been eating more, gaining weight, and losing her self-esteem.

She decides to apply this nine-step creative process by first formulating her intention, which is to feel secure, appreciated, and loved. She makes the commitment to read several popular books on relationships and is exposed to a number of new perspectives. She learns meditation, which she begins practicing regularly. During a particularly deep sitting, she has the insight that *she* has really been missing her friends, and her resentment stems from her husband's experiencing something that she would like for herself. She becomes inspired by the idea and makes plans to visit an old college roommate in another town. She so enjoys the few days that her entire attitude about her life completely shifts. She begins exercising and eating better and all her relationships, including her marriage, improve.

By setting up the conditions that allowed her

to experience a creative quantum leap, she was able to access life energy that was previously unavailable to her. This ability to experience new creative solutions to old problems is the essence of flexibility and a key component of reversing the aging process.

Opportunities for Creativity

Use the nine-step process every time you perceive a problem or challenge in your life. See every challenge as an opportunity for creativity. When you see every problem as an opportunity to practice the creative responses, you will look forward to and be excited by the challenges in your life.

Help others to solve their problems by teaching them the creative response. Teach and use the creative response at work and in your home life. Teach your children how to perceive their challenges as opportunities for creativity. Flexibility and creativity are the keys to evolutionary progress. Even in Darwinian terms, those who are able to adapt survive. Adaptation first requires flexibility, then creativity. Every evolutionary jump is a quantum leap in creativity. When you cultivate flexibility and practice the creative response you will notice how much younger, more flexible, and more adaptable you become.

Every day in every way,
I am increasing my mental and physical capacity.
My Biostat is set at a healthy ____ years of age.
I look and feel a healthy ____ years old.

I am reversing my biological age:

- *By changing my perception of my body, its aging and time;*
- *Through two kinds of deep rest—restful awareness and restful sleep;*
- *By nurturing my body through healthy foods;*
- *By using nutritional complements wisely;*
- *By enhancing mind/body integration;*
- *Through exercise;*
- *By eliminating toxins from my life; and*
- *By cultivating flexibility and creativity in consciousness.*

10

You Can Reverse Your Biological Age Through Love

ACTION STEP #9

I am reversing my biological age by making love the most important thing in my life.

I put this into practice by:

1. *Listening attentively and without interruption.*
2. *Expressing my appreciation to at least one person every day in an honest and sincere manner.*
3. *Consciously engaging in loving touch with those close to me, and becoming aware of my sexual energy in all its different expressions.*

Love heals.
Love renews.
Love makes you feel safe.
Love brings you closer to God.
Love conquers all fear.
Love makes you young.
Love reverses the aging process.

You can reverse your biological age through love. Love is the essence of life. For human beings, love is as essential as food and water, and without it, we cannot survive. Love is not just a psychological experience; love transforms biology. Mammalian babies from bunnies to chimpanzees fail to develop normally if they are deprived of their mother's love. Although we are not usually accustomed to considering love in scientific terms, over the past twenty-five years, scientific studies have provided indisputable evidence that the experience of love has profound life-supporting effects on our physiology.

Scientific studies show that by merely observing acts of compassion, your immunity is enhanced. David McClelland of Harvard University found that college students increase their production of salivary antibodies when watching a film of Mother Teresa comforting a child, whereas their antibody levels are depressed when watching war scenes. David Spiegel's studies from Stanford University have taught us that women facing metastatic cancer who participate in caring support groups live, on average, twice as long as those who do not. We know that men suffering heart attacks who believe that their wives love them do better than those who don't, and a simple monthly phone call from a caring cardiac nurse can double the survival time of a heart patient. Even studies with animals have found that tenderness and affection can reduce their risk for disease. In an intriguing study from Ohio State University, two groups of rabbits were fed a high-cholesterol diet. In one group the rabbits were regularly petted and cuddled by the animal technicians. Rabbits in the other group, fed the identical diet, did not receive any petting. At the completion of the study, the rabbits that were treated tenderly had only 10 percent as much fat deposited into their blood vessels as their touch-deficient peers. Love is metabolized into physiology and can make the difference between health and sickness, life and death.

These scientific reports do not surprise most of us. We have all known the exuberance and vitality that we experience when we feel loved. Most of us also know the anguish and despair that come from separation and rejection. People suffering the loss of love have changes in the chemistry of their brains that influence every cell in their body. These changes substantially increase their risk for a wide range of illnesses, from cancer to heart disease. Similarly, the exhilaration, enthusiasm, and comfort generated by love create life-affirming transformations that enliven both emotional and physical well-being. Love makes us feel good because it creates the biology of delight, joy, and safety. Love is healing, love is nourishing, love is good for us.

Love transforms biology.

What Is Love?

Knowing that love transforms our physiology in the direction of improved health and vitality, we are ready to address a fundamental question: What is love? Poets, philosophers, and songwriters since time immemorial have waxed eloquent on this perennial subject. No word in any language is embraced as personally as love. It elicits in each of us a lifetime of memories and desires, weaving together the innocence and passion of our bodies, hearts, and souls.

For most people, love is an emotion, a sentiment, a feeling that can consume your thoughts and molecules. Falling in love is an altered state of consciousness, in which your perceptions, interpretations, and choices are transformed. When you are in love you become carefree and open to new experiences. You become vulnerable and invincible at the same time. You become renewed, exhilarated, and joyful. Love detaches you from your usual mundane and trivial concerns and opens your awareness to the magic and mystery of life. Love reminds you that you are alive.

Love inspires you to do great things. Through the power of love you tap into your primordial energies and become a mythical being. Lovers aspire to epic undertakings to demonstrate the power of their love. Love connects you with archetypal lovers. You relish reenacting the recurrent love stories that precipitate out of the mythological realm of the human subconscious. Every culture tells its love stories. From Cupid and Psyche to Rama and Sita to Romeo and Juliet to Spencer Tracy and Katharine Hepburn, these romantic stories reenact the hell of separation and the heaven of reunion that human beings experience through love. These perennial love stories are the keys that open the door to universal love.

Personal Love as Concentrated Universal Love

The great spiritual traditions from every culture inform us that unity is the ultimate truth of all existence. The one undivided Spirit partitions itself into infinite beings. Once having fragmented, however, the parts are driven by fundamental forces to reestablish unity. Atoms endeavor to become molecules. Celestial bodies seek to join solar systems. Human beings strive to merge with their beloved. Love at its essence is the quest for spirit, and the longing for communion. The need to fulfill that longing for oneness resonates deep in our personal and collective memory. Through all the striving to find fullness outside ourselves, we know at some preconscious level that the only true source of love is the infinite, unbounded ocean of spirit within our own being. The more in touch with spirit we are, the more loving we feel and behave.

Most people are not directly in tune with their spiritual essence. Therefore, Nature, in her compassion for human beings, has provided the opportunity for us to fall in love with each other. This provides us a glimpse of the transformational power of spirit. Personal love provides us with a taste of universal love, but despite how grand we feel when we are in love, it is not enough. We are eternally driven to experience more love, more intimacy, more wonder because our soul is driven to experience the ultimate reunion with spirit.

When you recognize that love and spirit are

the same, you will see your longing for love as a hunger for more awareness, more communion, more connection with the universal intelligence that underlies the world. Every act of love is an act of divinity, an expression of spirit.

Make a commitment to see every act of love as an expression of spirit. A sweet look from a child, giving money to a homeless person, helping a stranger change a flat tire, bringing a spouse flowers, volunteering at a hospital—each of these acts is both personal and spiritual. They bring you greater joy by helping expand your concept of who you are. Every act of love loosens the shackle of ego imprisonment. Every act of love gives you a taste of spirit and brings you a step closer to integrating the timeless into time-bound existence. Love creates the experience of present-moment eternity, and the more we experience eternity the younger we grow. The deeper we tap into and express our core, which is spirit, the more loving and liberated we feel.

Think about love. Talk about love. Seek out love. Encourage love. Commit yourself to expressing love in every interaction of your life. This is the way your soul remembers its perfection. All lessons in life are lessons in love. Living a spiritual life means seeking out love in every situation. Make love the most important thing in your life and you will grow younger and live longer.

Love at its essence is the quest for spirit.

Communicating Love

Love is spirit in motion. Love moving from one heart to another generates the biology that reverses aging. Love has to be expressed in order for it to serve you and those you love. You can express your love for another person in three basic ways:

- You listen attentively to what they are saying.
- You express in words or actions your appreciation for them.
- You touch them lovingly with affection.

Each of these demonstrations of love happens spontaneously when you fall in love. Look at any couple smitten with love. They hang on each other's every word. They wax poetic about the things they find attractive, brilliant, and exceptional in each other. They express their appreciation through objects of love, from flowers to jewelry to homemade cookies. Finally, they cannot keep their hands off each other.

Whether you are in the first stages of a new romance, have been in a committed relationship for years, or are visiting an old friend from college, these three faces of love are important. Show your love by being fully present. Express your appreciation in words and deeds. Be affectionate. Consciously practice these principles of love. As a result, you will grow younger and live longer.

Love, Sex, and Spirit

Sexual energy is the primal creative energy of the universe, and all things that are alive arise from sexual energy. In animals and other life forms, sexual energy expresses itself exclusively as biological creativity. Animals beget more animals. In human beings, sexual energy can be channeled into creativity at all levels—physical, emotional, and spiritual. In any situation that makes you feel attraction, arousal, alertness, passion, interest, inspiration, excitement, creativity, or enthusiasm, sexual energy is at work.

All these different manifestations of sexual energy express themselves in your physical body as sensations. Whenever you are sexually aroused, there is an accompanying feeling in your body. Whenever you feel enthusiastic, inspired, joyful, energized, or passionate, there is also an accompanying feeling—a certain physical sensation. The common thread in each of these experiences is a feeling of expansion. At times the expansive feeling may be so strong that you feel you are bursting out of your skin. You are filled with energy. The medical term for this state of fullness is tumescence. Although it is usually applied to states of sexual arousal, it can also characterize these other expressions of excitement and passion.

Learn to get in touch with these sensations and recognize their various expressions in your body. Right now, close your eyes and recall an experience when you were passionately aroused by something. It may have been a beautiful piece of art, a breathtaking natural scene, or an emotionally moving piece of music. Perhaps it was when a brilliant business idea came to you, or when you heard something that gave you amazing insight into a problem you were facing. It may have been an erotic, passionate sexual experience. Notice the sensations that your inspirational experience generates in your body. This is the essence of sexual energy, which expresses itself in many different forms. Learn to recognize this powerful life force in all its manifestations.

Even as you go about your daily life, pay attention to these experiences of intense aliveness. They may be evoked by someone to whom you are intensely attracted, by a spectacular splash of color in the sky at sunset, or by seeing the beautiful, loving hands of your grandmother. Be aware of the empowering energy that is available to you as a passionate lover of life. Nurture these sensations with your attention until you feel a bubbling exuberance in every cell of your body. The more you look for and recognize these sensations in your body, the more your sensory experience will be one of heightened awareness, and the more you will experience a simple, unaffected appreciation and gratitude for the whole of creation. This is the essence of a spiritual life.

Despite what you may have been conditioned to believe, sexual desire is sacred and virtuous. It is the suppression of sexual energy that is artificial, unnatural, and contrived. For many people, the experience of sexual intimacy is their first glimpse into the experience of spirituality. When you and your beloved merge physically and emotionally, you go beyond the boundaries of the ego. In this state of union you experience timelessness, naturalness, playfulness, and defenselessness. These are qualities of spirit when it is not constrained by control, fear, or separation. Cultivating this state of natural openness and self-assured vulnerability in all relationships is the essence of a spiritual life.

SEXUAL VITALITY

Sexual energy is available to us at all ages. Being open to sexual energy reverses aging. Although many people have the impression that sexual energy diminishes as we age, studies have shown that the vast majority of both men and women are sexually active through their sixties, seventies, and beyond. About 90 percent of married men and women in their sixties and over 80 percent of men and women in their seventies are sexually active and find it enjoyable. Sexuality is a feature of intimate loving relationships throughout adult life.

There are physiological changes associated with aging that looked at from one angle can be viewed as a loss but from another perspective can be seen as an opportunity. Some men in their sixties and seventies take longer to become physically aroused. Some women need help compensating for tissue dryness that is associated with diminished estrogen production. These issues can be easily addressed. Investing the time and attention to create physical, emotional, and spiritual intimacy can often result in the most fulfilling sexual experiences of a person's life.

To improve your sexual experiences, you need to divest yourself of your expectations. Expectations are usually in three areas: (1) *performance,* as exemplified by the question "How am I doing?"; (2) *emotions,* as exemplified by the question "How am I feeling?"; and (3) *security,* as exemplified by the question "Do you really love me?" These are understandable concerns when exploring intimacy with your partner. They also provide a unique opportunity to express your vulnerabilities and create more intimacy. Intimacy derives from the willingness to be vulnerable. Ask for what you need and give to your lover what he or she needs. Openness, vulnerability, the willingness to give, and the readiness to receive are all qualities of spirit.

Relinquish your expectations. When you relinquish your expectations, you are able to release your resistance. Your resistance keeps you from enjoying what is happening. In sex, as in all areas of life, resistance is born of fear. All resistance is mental and derives from a judgment against what is being felt. Practice releasing your judgments and releasing your expectations and you will experience the passion and surrender that sex offers. The concentrated passion of sexual lovemaking then permeates all other aspects of your life.

If you find that sex is mixed with hidden emotions such as shame, guilt, or anger, commit to releasing these toxic and inhibiting feelings. Sexual intimacy is one road to the experience of true freedom, because it is one area of life in which you can become completely uninhibited and free. Sexual fulfillment occurs when the experience comes from playfulness instead of need. When sex is used to fulfill needs, it leads to addiction. When sex comes from playfulness, the result is ecstasy.

Despite what you may have been conditioned to believe, sexual desire is sacred and virtuous.

For Play

Sex is most enjoyable and creates the greatest amount of love and intimacy when it is viewed as a process rather than as a goal. Western society is dominated by a goal-oriented worldview. Both men and women are conditioned to achieve whatever goal is established, as directly, quickly, and efficiently as possible. This attitude plays itself out in our lovemaking where we've learned to prize sexual climax as the sole target of physical intimacy. Although every lover relishes the pleasure of orgasm, the ancient wisdom traditions of India and China suggest that playing with sexual energy and extending the process of lovemaking expands the heart, mind, and spirit, while intensely enriching physical delight. Known as Tantra in India and the Tao of Sex in traditional Chinese culture, the basic principles for conscious lovemaking include *ritual, communication,* and *finesse.*

Ritual

If you view sex as a sacred act, you will understand the value of ritual. Take the time to prepare yourself for lovemaking as if you were journeying to a realm of celestial pleasure. Bathe yourself and prepare your body and mind for the sharing of your most personal gifts. Set the lovemaking scene with attention to all the senses. Read inspiring love poems to your partner. Play beautiful music that arouses your passions and opens your heart. (See appendix for our recommendations.) Wear sensual clothing, employ subtle lighting with candles, and diffuse pleasing aromas in the room. Look into your lover's eyes and silently or aloud acknowledge the gift of engaging intimately with your partner.

When you consider sexuality as simply another

physiological need, it only serves that purpose. Recognizing that unlike your animal ancestors, you have the ability to channel creative sexual energy to expand your heart and raise your consciousness, you can use rituals to focus your attention and intention. Transforming an exchange between two people from an act of pure biology to one of body, mind, and spirit generates passion, vitality, and ecstasy.

COMMUNICATION

Communicate your feelings and needs to your partner, before, during, and after sex. Express what brings you pleasure and what you need to feel safe, adored, and aroused. Reorient your intention from simply releasing sexual pressure to celebrating the process. Prolonging the act of lovemaking has energy-enhancing effects on mind and body. Inform your partner when you are about to climax and slow down the tempo to expand and prolong the pleasure. Lovemaking is a dance of body, mind, and soul that can continue twenty-four hours a day in physical, emotional, and spiritual domains.

Sexual ecstasy is nourished through your willingness to be vulnerable. Asking for what you need to fulfill your deepest desires and fantasies requires your willingness to be vulnerable.

Through this vulnerability the boundaries between "I" and "thou" and between body and soul become blurred. This is the essence of a spiritual experience and the promise of conscious lovemaking.

Finesse

Like meditation, lovemaking is a domain where force, effort, and control fail to result in success and fulfillment. Subtlety, timing, and finesse are the essence of rapturous lovemaking. The blossoming of sexual bliss requires total attention in the present moment and openness to creativity. Sex can be a tool for personal transformation when you listen to the signals from your body and the body of your lover and use them to surrender and release your resistance and fear. Lovemaking provides access to personal, collective, and universal domains of awareness. Every loving couple is reenacting the perennial myths of love; every loving couple is reenacting the reunion of souls. In Traditional Chinese Medicine, lovemaking is an opportunity for the primordial inward moving (yin) and outward moving (yang) forces to balance. In Ayurveda and Tantra, sexual union is the personalized expression of the eternal dance between the impulses of pure potentiality (Shiva) and creative expression (Shakti).

True intimacy is union between flesh and flesh, between heart and heart, between soul and soul. Sexual energy is the creative energy of the universe. Sexual energy is sacred energy. When we have restored the sexual experience to the realm of the sacred, our world becomes divine, holy, and healed.

Through the vulnerability of sexual intimacy,
the boundaries between "I" and "thou"
and between body and soul become blurred.

Ojas—the Essence of Love

You have been using the mantra ojas in your daily ritual to perceive your body as a field of energy, transformation, and intelligence. This subtle substance is nourishing to your physical, emotional, and spiritual bodies. It provides the integrating essence that unifies all aspects of your being.

According to Ayurveda, we are born with a small reserve of ojas that can be augmented or depleted as a result of nourishing or toxic experiences. Healthy food, loving emotions, nurturing sensory impressions, rejuvenating herbs, and creative use of sexual energy all contribute to more abundant ojas. Ojas reminds every cell in the body of its primary directive to support the wholeness of the mind/body network. It also strengthens your natural immunity. When ojas is depleted you become susceptible to degenerative disorders including cancer. Therefore, protecting and increasing your supply of ojas is key to reversing the aging process.

Ojas can be depleted by excessive release of reproductive fluid. This is important in men and forms the basis of the idea that as you age, reducing the frequency of ejaculation can improve your vitality. This suggestion is not based upon morality; rather, it is an expression of the conservation of energy. As a general principle, if you are male, see if you can increase the ratio of sexual experiences to ejaculation. If you are accustomed to releasing sexual tension every time you have sex, see if you can go to an every other time pattern. Then try going to every third time. Although at first you may feel some sense of frustration, you will most likely quickly begin to appreciate the enhanced energy and passion that you feel throughout the day. If you are a woman, play with your partner to keep his sexual energy aroused without immediately releasing it. When lovers consciously direct their powerful sexual energy, they become more attractive to each other. All aspects of lovemaking, in and outside of its sexual expression, become more ecstatic.

Nutrition for Ojas

According to Ayurveda there are special foods and herbs that have distinctive ojas-enhancing effects. Fresh fruits and vegetables, whole grains, nuts (particularly almonds), honey, and dairy derived from well-cared-for cows are all enhancing to ojas. Substances depleting ojas include alcohol, tobacco, canned foods, highly processed foods, fried foods, and those containing artificial sweeteners. Make your healthier choices without being overly compulsive or rigid. Compulsivity and rigidity deplete ojas. Simply be more conscious of your choices so that to the extent possible, you increase the ojas in your life.

Herbs and Ojas

There are many classical rejuvenative herbs from healing systems around the world that can be considered ojas-enhancing. Ginseng from the Chinese and Korean systems is the most popular herb in the world and has been classically used to augment sexual potency. Scientific studies have suggested that ginseng can enhance sexual appetite and erectile function in both animals and men. It can enhance your general sense of well-being and vitality. Ginseng is available in many forms including capsules, teas, and even chewing gum.

Ayurveda has an entire branch of medicine dedicated to maintaining and regaining optimal reproductive tissue. Known as *Vajikarana,* these herbs are sometimes referred to as aphrodisiacs. Although you most likely think of an aphrodisiac as something that arouses sexual desires, according to Ayurveda, these aphrodisiac herbs also improve your reproductive essence. In other words, they enhance ojas. The three most commonly recommended ojas-enhancing substances in Ayurveda are ashwagandha, shatavari, and amalaki.

Ashwagandha (Withania somnifera)

Sometimes known as winter cherry, this potently fragrant herb has long been known as the primary masculine rejuvenating substance. Its Sanskrit name means "smelling like a stallion," implying that it infuses the user with the power of a horse. Although its long-standing reputation is as a sexual potency herb, most research has focused on its stress-reducing and immune-enhancing properties. A recent experiment with animals found that ashwagandha influences the pituitary chemicals that regulate sex hormones.

Ayurveda recommends taking a teaspoon of ashwagandha in warm milk sweetened with honey or brown sugar before bedtime. This is highly encouraged on days when the man has ejaculated, with the intention of helping to replenish lost ojas. It is equally valuable for women to enliven their passion and sexual ardor. Ashwagandha is now readily available from a number of herbal distributors in the West.

Shatavari (Asparagus racemosus)

This wild form of asparagus is considered to be the feminine equivalent of ashwagandha in that it supports the nurturing, receptive, creative feminine energy that both men and women possess. Not known for understatement, Ayurveda gives this nourishing plant the Sanskrit name shatavari, which can be translated as "capable of supporting one hundred husbands." It is a classical tonic with several indications including relief of premenstrual symptoms, enhancement of milk flow in breastfeeding mothers, and the smoothing of the transition through menopause. Scientific studies on shatavari have been limited to date, primarily looking into its traditional role in relieving stomach upset and improving lactation. Considering its long-standing history of value in strengthening a woman's physiology, shatavari is worthy of further scientific exploration.

Although most commonly recommended for women, shatavari is also considered a valuable tonic for men. Like ashwagandha, it is usually taken in hot milk sweetened with honey or raw sugar. The combination of shatavari and ashwagandha (one teaspoon of each) in a cup of hot milk with a pinch of saffron and a little honey or brown sugar makes an excellent tonic for both men and women and is a traditional ojas restorer.

Amalaki (Emblica officinalis)

The powerful little fruit is one of nature's most abundant sources of antioxidants. Ounce per ounce, amalaki juice carries twenty times the vitamin C content of orange juice. Amalaki is considered the most powerful general Ayurvedic tonic, beneficial for both men and women. It is most readily available in the West in the form of an herbal jam that combines amalaki with a number of other tonic herbs and spices.

The mythology around this ancient rejuvenating substance describes an elderly sage, Chavan, who was asked by a king to marry his daughter. Chavan was concerned that he would not be able to satisfy the needs of his young bride, but in meditation cognized the herbal formula that would restore his youthful vitality. This subsequently became know as Chavanprash or the jam of Chavan.

Scientific research on amalaki has shown it to have measurable health-enhancing properties, including the detoxification of carcinogens, protection of DNA, lowering of cholesterol levels and relief of heartburn. Amalaki-based herbal jams are becoming increasingly available in the West. We recommend a teaspoon or two each day as a natural, general ojas-enhancing tonic. Sources of ashwagandha, shatavari, and amalaki jam are listed in the appendix.

When we have restored the sexual experience
to the realm of the sacred,
our world becomes divine, holy, and healed.

The Soul of Love

Love serves the soul. We learn our life lessons and awaken our memory of wholeness through love. Our soul is the weaving of our memories and desires, providing the template for all our aspirations, choices, and experiences in life. We can look at the soul as a confluence of contexts and meaning. Context entails a set of relationships and meaning is the way we interpret the relationships. Our lives are a river of relationships and meaning.

Each of us is continuously reenacting one of the perennial themes of love—trust and betrayal, unrequited love and forbidden lust, unconditional love and calculating neediness. From Adam and Eve to Judas and Jesus, the most powerful stories we tell each other across time and culture are love stories. Love is the primal force on earth and beyond all the obvious and stated reasons, behind every action is love. Striving for good grades in school, doing well in a job, creating a great work of art, composing a beautiful symphony, writing a great novel, winning the Nobel Prize—if you dig deeply enough you will see that all these stories are love stories in disguise. In actuality, the only reason we do anything is for more love, although we may go to considerable lengths to conceal our true motivations.

Our discussion of love leads to a simple conclusion: For the benefit of your physical, emotional, and spiritual well-being, generate more love in your life. Each morning when you awaken, ask yourself, "How can I create more love today? How can I express more love today? How can I be open to receiving more love today?" In every interaction ensure that some exchange of love takes place. Whether it is chatting with your landscaper, paying for your groceries, talking with your children or being intimate with your beloved, come from an inner dialogue of love. When you make love the most important thing in your life, your mind and body resonate with the timeless.

Every day in every way,
I am increasing my mental and physical capacity.
My Biostat is set at a healthy ____ years of age.
I look and feel a healthy ____ years old.

I am reversing my biological age:

- *By changing my perception of my body, its aging and time;*
- *Through two kinds of deep rest—restful awareness and restful sleep;*
- *By nurturing my body through healthy foods;*
- *By using nutritional complements wisely;*
- *By enhancing mind/body integration;*
- *Through exercise;*
- *By eliminating toxins from my life;*
- *By cultivating flexibility and creativity in consciousness; and*
- *Through love.*

11

You Can Reverse Your Biological Age by Maintaining a Youthful Mind

ACTION STEP #10

I am reversing my biological age by maintaining a youthful mind.

I put this into practice by:

1. *Enriching my sensory experience, within and without.*
2. *Devoting myself to lifelong learning and personal growth.*
3. *Enjoying play, lightheartedness, and laughter.*

The body is a field of molecules.
The mind is a field of ideas.
Wherever a thought goes a molecule goes.
Fresh and youthful thoughts
create fresh and youthful molecules.
Psychological age influences biological age.

The tenth step to grow younger and live longer is to maintain a youthful mind. The mind is not a thing, as the body is. The body is a field of molecules. You can touch it. It is solid. Even though it is constantly and ever in change and transformation, it has the appearance of a fixed object, like a sculpture. We can examine the body, and measure its biological markers in a fairly precise, objective way. These biomarkers were discussed in Chapter 1.

The mind on the other hand is not a field of molecules; it is a field of ideas. Ideas cannot be put in a test tube or observed through a microscope. They cannot be examined in the traditional objective sense. Ideas can only be experienced subjectively. According to Ayurveda, the body is a field of information and energy that we experience objectively, and the mind is the same field of information and energy that we experience subjectively. There is a correlation between subjectivity and objectivity. Wherever a thought goes, a molecule goes.

Spiritual traditions say that the word was made

into flesh. In reality, the word and the flesh are the same thing, much as physics tells us that particles and waves are the same thing. The body is a collection of particles. The mind is a collection of waves. They are the same thing experienced differently, depending on your method of observation—objective or subjective.

Many studies have confirmed that biological age correlates better with psychological age than chronological age. If you are young at heart, your biological markers are likely to reflect a young heart, literally. When your heart is being attacked through hostility or lack of love, you might indeed suffer a heart attack.

It therefore becomes important to understand what creates a youthful mind, because a youthful mind is likely to translate into a youthful body. All the factors we have discussed in the preceding chapters are, of course, very important. However, if your mind is old, your body will reflect it even if you practice everything that we have suggested so far in this book. A youthful mind is a mind that is constantly growing. As a popular saying goes, "People don't grow old. When they stop growing, they become old."

Neuroscientists are learning that the brain is an extraordinarily dynamic organ that is continuously reshaping itself. The cortex of the brain, which is less than one-quarter of an inch thick and covers only 350 square inches, contains over 20 billion neurons. Each of these brain cells has over 10,000 connections with other nerve cells throughout the brain. These connections are undergoing constant transformation. The electrical, magnetic, and chemical fields of your brain are in perpetual flux, reflecting your moment-to-moment changing experiences.

Even the anatomy of your brain is being resculpted. Microscopic tendrils connecting one neuron with another are extending and retracting. The cells themselves are coming and going. The long-standing belief that adults never generate new brain cells has been overturned. Recently, researchers at Princeton University have found evidence that thousands of fresh brain cells are born every day.

Your experiences are ever changing. All experiences take place in the mind, which is notoriously nonstationary. The brain reflects this pliability. Attend to keeping your mind fresh and youthful, and you will keep your brain and your body fresh and youthful.

The body is a field of information and
energy that we experience objectively;
the mind is the same field of
information and energy that
we experience subjectively.

A Youthful Mind

A youthful mind is dynamic, vibrant, and curious. This is what we all desire—an alert vibrant mind along with strong physical vitality. As a result of your commitment to the other steps in this program, you have set the stage for this ideal state. You have changed your perceptions and expectations about aging. You are taking time on a daily basis to quiet your mind through meditation. You are lovingly nurturing your body with healthy food, nutritional complements, mind/body integration techniques, and balanced exercise. You are eliminating toxins from your body, mind, and soul. You are cultivating flexibility and creativity in your consciousness, and you are making love the most important thing in your life. With all these other key components in place, it is essential that you keep your mind active and expanding so you can enjoy the fruits of the life-affirming choices you've made and the life wisdom you have accumulated.

A youthful mind has many vital qualities. It is enthusiastic, it is spontaneous, it is fluid, and it is adaptable. Observe a child at ease and you will see all the qualities of a youthful mind in action. You have a youthful mind within you now. You simply need to allow its expression.

Enthusiasm

A youthful mind is an enthusiastic mind. The word *enthusiasm* comes from the Greek word *entheos,* meaning "filled with the divine." A mind that is infused with the creative intelligence of the cosmos is a youthful mind. It is overflowing with energy. The universe is born anew every moment, and a mind that resonates with this energy sees the world with the wide-eyed enthusiasm of a child. Follow the advice of Lord Shiva who encourages you to "step out of the river of memory and conditioning and see the world as if for the first time."

A youthful mind is a beginner's mind. It is enthusiastic about everything—a butterfly, a rainbow, the stars at night, a cottontail rabbit, a new book, a fragrant rose, a fresh strawberry. Stay alert to the amazing display that is taking place around you. Pay attention to the remarkable dance of nature that is ever fresh and new. Energized alertness is the basis of enthusiasm. Enthusiasm reverses aging.

Spontaneity

A youthful mind is spontaneous. It is unpredictable. It has not been conditioned. A youthful mind is awake to all possibilities and is not inhibited by established norms. A youthful mind relinquishes the need to narrowly define itself. A youthful mind tolerates ambiguity, which gives rise to spontaneity.

You have spontaneous impulses inside of you right now. Close your eyes and feel the exuberance of spontaneity that wants to manifest. Right now, as you are reading this book, do something spontaneous. Find the impulse within you and nourish it with your attention. Here are some suggestions:

- Kiss your spouse
- Start dancing
- Call your mother
- Start singing
- Take off your clothes
- Read a poem
- Draw a picture

Be spontaneous. It is not possible to "practice" spontaneity, but you can be alert to nurturing the spontaneous impulses that are bubbling up inside of you. Spontaneity is a quality of a youthful mind.

Fluidity and Adaptability

A youthful mind is fluid and adaptable. It does not allow itself to be trapped by boundaries that overshadow the unity of all things. It naturally sees the interrelatedness of life, and therefore is able to flow with changing situations and circumstances without resistance. A youthful mind does not get stuck in fine distinctions.

Be adaptable. Don't allow yourself to get trapped into viewing things from a narrow, limited perspective. Practice seeing the big picture. Avoid letting boundaries overshadow your unity. Look for the interrelatedness of all things in life.

Your Quantum Mind

At the level of quantum reality, the universe is not made up of things. It is comprised of oscillating fields of energy. The quantum domain is spontaneous. It is inherently unpredictable, resisting all efforts to define it precisely. In the quantum domain, everything is interrelated. Any perturbation in the field influences everything else in the field.

The quantum realm has unlimited energy, unlimited unpredictability, and unlimited interconnectedness. Another way of saying this is that the quantum realm is enthusiastic, spontaneous, and fluid. These are the qualities of the cosmic mind that every moment gives rise to a fresh universe. These are the qualities of a youthful mind that every moment gives rise to a new body.

Heightening Your Level of Sensory Awareness

A youthful mind is alert to the rich inner and outer sensations of life. An aged mind is dull and oblivious to the sensory delights that are available internally and externally. You can create a youthful, exuberant mind by heightening your state of sensory awareness. Awaken to the rich sensations inside and outside of you. Enliven your imagination. A youthful mind is tuned in to the multidimensional, multisensory universe we inhabit.

Nourishing Your Body/Mind Through the Five Senses

Pay attention to your environment. Feed your senses delectable, interesting, awe-inspiring impulses. A youthful mind is nourished through the exploration of new domains. See your environment with fresh eyes. Don't take your world for granted.

- Listen to beautiful, interesting, different music from around the world. Listen to the sounds of nature—birds singing, the wind blowing through the leaves, rain beating on your roof, ocean waves crashing against the shore.
- Feel the texture of things. Dig your hands into the earth. Stroke your pet. Caress your loved ones. Feel a sculpture. Rub your hands along a tree's bark.
- Look at your world with fresh eyes. Notice things you don't usually pay attention to. Look at the many shades of green that nature paints. Watch the clouds manifest and dissolve. Go to your local art museum and walk through the galleries. Really look at the faces of the people in your life.
- Taste things as if for the first time. Bite into a tart apple. Savor the flavor of freshly baked cherry pie. Pop a clove bud in your mouth. Taste your lover with a passionate kiss. Drink a freshly squeezed glass of orange juice. Delight your taste buds.
- Notice the aromas in your environment. Breathe in the fragrances of your garden. Sniff the smells of dinner. Inhale the scents of your

loved one. Go outside after a rain and smell the earth. Notice how closely smells are linked with your memories and emotions.

Expand Your Imagination

The energy and information of the world is translated into subtle sensory impulses that are experienced on the screen of your consciousness. These inner impulses are known in Ayurveda as *Tanmatras.* We can think of them as mental quanta, the subjective equivalent to the subtlest units of matter in the physical world. Awakening the Tanmatras through active imagination creates a youthful mind.

Read the following visualizations, then close your eyes and invoke a vivid impression in your mind.

Sound

Imagine the sound of:

- A church bell tolling on Sunday morning
- A cricket, chirping outside your window at night
- A marching band performing at a high school football game
- A grandfather clock sounding six o'clock
- A coyote howling at the moon

Touch

Imagine the sensations of:

- Walking on a sandy beach
- Taking a hot shower
- Touching a rose petal
- Stroking the soft cheek of an infant child
- Caressing satin sheets

Vision

Imagine the sight of:

- The sun setting over the Pacific Ocean
- A flock of geese flying in formation overhead
- Cumulus clouds on a warm summer day
- A children's ballet performance
- An Olympic diver jumping off the platform

Taste

Imagine the taste of:

- A fresh, ripe peach
- A spoonful of chocolate-chip ice cream
- Gargling with mint-flavored mouthwash
- A pungent jalapeño pepper
- A bitter leaf of endive lettuce

Smell

Imagine the smell of:

- Bread baking in the oven
- A new bar of sandalwood soap
- A cinnamon stick
- A freshly cut lemon
- A fragrant rose

Multisensory Imagination

You can develop your subtle senses by imagining multisensory experiences. Start with the following exercises and then create your own visualizations to exercise your imagination.

Imagine:

You are walking along the beach on a tropical island. You feel the warm sun on your body. You hear the ocean waves lapping at the shore and the call of seagulls. You smell the faint waft of your coconut suntan lotion.

Imagine:

You are in a late-fifties diner. The sounds of an Elvis Presley song fill the room from the jukebox in the corner. The young men in the restaurant are wearing white T-shirts with their sleeves rolled up. You take your first swallow of the chocolate milk shake served in a large frosty fountain glass.

Imagine:

You are lying on a lounge chair on a warm summer night. Fireflies are glowing on and off as you gaze into the dark sky. Crickets are chirping in unison. The fragrance of night-blooming jasmine perfuses the air. As you take a bite out of a fresh peach, a shooting star flashes through the sky.

Nurture the enthusiasm that comes with heightened awareness of the sounds, sensations, sights, tastes, and smells in your outer and inner worlds. Pay attention to the gifts your senses bring you.

Learning and Growing

A youthful mind is a growing mind. It is dedicated to continual expansion and learning. A youthful mind thrives on new experiences and new knowledge. Experience combined with knowledge leads to wisdom.

Make a commitment to learn throughout your life. Here are just a few suggestions to keep your mind growing:

- Read—the classics, novels, Shakespeare, science fiction, fantasies. Try genres you do not usually choose.
- Read poetry—Rumi, Tagore, Hafiz, Blake, Longfellow, Frost, Ginsburg, and the modern poets
- Read spiritual literature—the Bible, the Koran, the Bhagavad Gita, the Upanishads, the Dhammapada
- Take classes at your local college
- Learn a foreign language
- Take piano lessons
- Learn to dance
- Take art classes
- Learn to cook
- Take writing classes
- Join a choir
- Take pottery classes
- Learn a new computer program
- Take a poetry-writing class
- Go to workshops—on love, on human potential, on success, on spirituality, on health
- Take horseback-riding lessons
- Take a photography class
- Visit new places
- Travel to foreign lands
- Go to museums and art galleries
- Watch foreign films
- Go to concerts

Relinquish rigid ideas about who you are, and challenge yourself with new experiences and new perspectives. Expand your vocabulary. Keep abreast of trends in art, science, technology, medicine, politics, music, and fashion. Don't be afraid to question prevailing beliefs, including your own. Learn something new every day. As you continue stimulating your mind to grow, your brain will continue creating new connections among its billions of cells.

Experience combined with knowledge leads to wisdom.

Playfulness, Lightheartedness, and Laughter

A youthful mind is playful and lighthearted. It laughs easily, genuinely, and with abandon. You can probably recall times from your childhood when you giggled so hard you could barely stand or walk. Playfulness and joy are qualities of Spirit, which is inherently lighthearted. Knowing itself as eternal and unbounded, Spirit does not surrender its magic and enthusiasm for trivial concerns.

Play and recreation go hand in hand. Play is literally an opportunity for re-*creation*—an opportunity to re-create yourself. When you play with abandon, you enter into the present moment. You let go of the past and forget about the future. When you are playing, you lose track of time. The timeless domain of play is the realm of Spirit. Spirit is innately playful.

The ego, on the other hand, is serious. It is solely concerned with power, control, and approval. The ego is easily offended. Whatever arrogance or self-importance people may project, if they are dominated by their ego, their underlying experience is one of fear—fear of losing control, fear of losing power, fear of losing approval. This fear leads to seriousness and the tendency to be easily offended.

When you shift your internal reference from ego to spirit, you relinquish your need to control, cajole, withhold, seduce, and manipulate and simply allow the universe and life to unfold. This creates a natural state of ease, which predisposes you to lightheartedness and laughter.

Laughter is the best medicine for body and mind. Scientific studies have shown that laughter can enliven the immune system, raise pain thresholds and ease depression. We encourage you to have the intention to lighten up and be open to the wonder and delight of living a human life. Remind yourself, remind your friends, and remind your loved ones not to allow terminal seriousness to consume the life force.

Suggestions for Playfulness and Laughter

- Spend time with children
- Go to toy stores
- Play with your animals
- Go to an improvisational theater show
- Watch funny movies
- Go to a comedy store
- Rent old *Candid Camera* episodes
- Watch Marx Brothers movies
- Go to the beach
- Take a ski trip
- Watch *I Love Lucy* reruns
- Ride your bicycle
- Go bowling
- Rent Rollerblades
- Go to a baseball game
- Start a pillow fight
- Tell jokes
- Play board games
- Tickle someone
- Have a staring contest
- Throw a costume party
- Go to an animal-free circus
- Dance
- Have a tea party
- Go to an ice cream shop
- Bake cookies
- Blow bubbles

- Play miniature golf
- Go to the batting cages
- Watch people at shopping malls
- Go to an amusement park
- Paint with watercolors
- Rent a sailboat
- Go on a picnic
- Make up lists of fun and playful things to do

The timeless domain of play is the realm of Spirit. Spirit is innately playful.

According to Vedic science, the purpose of life is the expansion of happiness. Creation is a marvelous divine play that assigns each of us a different role. The Sanskrit word for this play is *leela.* You can take your role very seriously and miss life's magic, or you can recognize that you are eternal Spirit disguising yourself as an actor and celebrate the leela. Not taking life or yourself too seriously does not mean being irresponsible. In actuality, if you recognize the cosmic play you become more responsible, for you see every thought, word, and action as an expression of the divine playwright. Relish the magic and the mystery in every moment.

Laughter is a symptom of spirituality. Laughter

is the flow of love, coursing through your body. Laughter is the nectar of present-moment awareness.

Invite more enthusiasm into your life.
Invite more playfulness.
Invite more lightheartedness.
Invite more laughter.

One of our favorite playful and lighthearted cosmic revelers is the fourteenth-century mystic Hafiz, whose poems have been translated recently by Daniel Ladinsky. Hafiz invites us all to join in the cosmic dance.

What is laughter?
What is this precious love and laughter
Budding in our hearts?
It is the glorious sound
Of a soul waking up!

Play and enjoy. It will keep you young in body, mind, and soul.

Every day in every way,
I am increasing my mental and physical capacity.
My Biostat is set at a healthy ____ years of age.
I look and feel a healthy ____ years old.

I am reversing my biological age:

- *By changing my perception of my body, its aging and time;*
- *Through two kinds of deep rest—restful awareness and restful sleep;*
- *By nurturing my body through healthy foods;*
- *By using nutritional complements wisely;*
- *By enhancing mind/body integration;*
- *Through exercise;*
- *By eliminating toxins from my life;*
- *By cultivating flexibility and creativity in consciousness;*
- *Through love; and*
- *By maintaining a youthful mind.*

Epilogue

In James Hilton's classic 1933 work *Lost Horizon,* the central character, Hugh Conway, unexpectedly finds himself in a remote Tibetan land called Shangri-La. He soon discovers that the inhabitants of this domain are playing by a different set of rules, for sickness, aging, and death are rare phenomena. The high lama of the monastery, for example, informs Conway that as a result of secret antiaging practices, he has been alive for more than two hundred and fifty years!

Soon after arriving, Conway finds himself attracted to Lo-Tsen, an enchanting nineteen-year-old Chinese girl who plays music each evening for the resident monks. He eventually learns that the girl longs to escape from Shangri-La. Despite her comfortable existence in paradise, she yearns for the experience of contrast that Shangri-La, with its absence of suffering, aging, and death, cannot provide.

Conway, his younger associate, and Lo-Tsen leave Shangri-La on a treacherous journey back to civilization. We do not learn their fate until the epilogue, when it is revealed that Conway has been brought to a mission hospital in China by an old, frail woman, who immediately succumbs to a feverish illness. Leaving Shangri-La has unmasked the woman's real age, which is over a hundred years old. We are left only to imagine the ultimate destiny of Hugh Conway.

As long as human beings have existed, we have dreamt of lands like Shangri-La. We envision these domains as exotic places with lush valleys, beautiful natural scenery, and pure mountain air. And yet Shangri-La is not a place. It is a state of consciousness in which one lives in a timeless reality, where all material things are experienced as endless transformations of energy and intelligence, where suffering, aging, entropy, and even death do not exist.

While such a place may at first seem desirable, the story of Shangri-La reminds us that as human beings we require contrast, meaning, and purpose for our lives to be worth living. Osho tells the story of a man who dreams that immediately upon his arrival at a celestial plane, an attendant informs him that anything he desires will instantly manifest. The man asks for a meal and the attendant instantaneously creates a sumptuous feast for him. The man asks for entertainment and the attendant immediately conjures up a band of actors and musicians to amuse him. He expresses sensual yearning and beautiful women are instantly manifested to indulge his sexual fantasies. Although he is initially fascinated with his experience, after a few days the man becomes bored and asks the attendant if he can provide some work for him to do. The attendant politely informs him that he can give the man anything he wants except purposeful activity. The man replies, "I cannot spend all my time without something useful to do. I might as well be in Hell!" to which the attendant replies, "Where do you think you are?"

According to Ayurveda, human life span depends upon our collective consciousness. In Vedic mythology, human consciousness goes through four cycles, known in Sanskrit as *yugas.* In each yuga, the life span of human beings changes. In the first cycle, known as *Sat Yuga,* 75 percent of people are living enlightened lives, and therefore most people live a very long time. If we are to believe the Old Testament, people, as exemplified by Methuselah, can live to a thousand years of age in Sat Yuga.

The second yuga is called *Dwarpa Yuga.* In this

age about 50 percent of people are in a higher state of consciousness. In Dwarpa Yuga the average life span is purported to be about 500 years. The third cycle of time is called *Treta Yuga.* In this age 25 percent of people are in higher states of consciousness and the average life span is supposed to be 250 years.

Finally, we come to the fourth cycle, known as *Kala Yuga,* in which only a handful of people are experiencing higher states of consciousness. According to Ayurveda, this is our current age. But even in Kala Yuga, the average life span is supposed to be a hundred years, so most human beings are not even reaching their full potential in Kala Yuga. This stage is sometimes referred to as the age of darkness because people are experiencing such a small fraction of their vast mental and physical potential.

Critics may dismiss these theories as part of mythology, but as Joseph Campbell, the distinguished explorer of mythology, once said, "Mythology contains more truth than history." Mythology expresses the greatest aspirations, desires, and ambitions of the collective imagination. The time may be coming when we can fulfill these aspirations. The theory of collective consciousness states that if just 1 percent of people were experiencing higher states of consciousness, there would be a completely different expression of society. Everything would change: the crime rate would plummet, hospital admissions would fall, and people would live healthier and longer lives.

After billions of years of evolution, life is beginning to divulge its innermost secrets. Biological intelligence carried in the genetic code has created a human being that is now capable of exploring its own origins. Modern scientists, unraveling the human genome, are deciphering the alphabet of life. We all hope that with this new technology we will better understand and intervene in illness and aging. Technology itself is neutral—it is neither inherently good nor bad. How we use technology is a reflection of our collective consciousness.

As the science of genetics evolves, we may be able to substantially extend life and ensure that more and more people are able to live out their full potential. It is critical that we raise our awareness so we can collectively make choices that are most evolutionary for individuals, the human species, and the global ecology. Jonas Salk, the great biologist and developer of the first polio vaccine, expressed the brilliant insight that if we are to survive as a species, we must move beyond the Darwinian concept of "survival of the fittest" to a new paradigm: "survival of the wisest." The principles and practices offered in this book are dedicated to such a high purpose.

The cycle of life is one of continuous transformation. Adaptation leads to stability, which eventually results in stagnation, entropy, disintegration, dissolution, and incubation (commonly perceived of as death). In the right season, incubation gives rise to a quantum leap in creativity, experienced as rebirth, resurrection, and renewal. Without this unending cycle we would be doomed to eternal senility.

Our collective beliefs, expectations, and choices have been such that the forces of decay and entropy have dominated our experience of life. It is time to turn our attention to the creative forces within us. While the cycle will continue, we believe that as the next few decades unfold, we will see a new era in which human aging will have a completely new expression. As you have learned by now from this book, it is possible to have increased vitality, creativity, and mental and physical capacity as the years unroll. Many have lamented that youth is wasted on the young, but now we have the opportunity to experience the exquisite combination of mature wisdom along with youthful biology. Through our interpretation and choices we can increase both the quality and quantity of human life, adding both years to our life and life to our years. This should be our intention for the world and ourselves.

We have access to Shangri-La in our own awareness. Modern physicists tell us that quantum mathematics predicts parallel coexisting realities. In the quantum world there are no fixed objects, only superpositions of probability—oscillating fields of possibility. Shangri-La is one such possibility—a projection of consciousness that is beyond the limitations of time and space. The world of disease, decay, entropy, and premature death is another projection of consciousness that is currently our pervasive one. When reality shifts, both the observer and the observed change. The observer in one reality is quite different from the observer in another; if the observer does not change, neither does the observed.

Here the observed is the body while the observer is your state of consciousness. Although focusing on the body through diet, exercise, and herbs can be helpful, the real shift has to be in consciousness. When you, the observer, shifts, your body also shifts, and your interpretation of your life transforms. One consequence of this transformation is the recognition that aging is a choice.

According to Ayurveda, every human being is a weaving together of the environment, body, mind, and spirit. The environment has the shortest shelf life, for it is changing every moment. The body has a slightly longer shelf life. It takes about a year to replace almost all the atoms and molecules that comprise it. The mind, which includes the intellect and ego, has a still longer shelf life. Your aspirations, beliefs, dreams, memories, and desires may last an entire lifetime. Your soul is eternal and not subject to the entropy and decay that govern the environment, body, and mind. Live your life from the level of your soul and you will be timeless.

This awareness will not do away with the essential fact of your physical mortality. The soul must have the opportunity to evolve and take quantum leaps in creativity. To live in the same body forever would be like getting stuck with the same automobile for eternity. At some point, the old must give rise to the new. The cycle must go on as beautifully expressed in the Alfred, Lord Tennyson poem:

The old order changeth, yielding place to new;
And God fulfills himself in many ways,

Lest one good custom should corrupt
the world.

We have given you the tools in this book to become a co-creator with God to harness the evolutionary forces of imagination, inspiration, innovation, and creativity. There is immense power in these tools. We hope you will use them wisely and, by example, lead the way in helping to create a world of joy, wisdom, and vitality.

Grow Younger, Live Longer Recipes

The following are seven vegetarian menus of worldwide regional cuisine. (All the following recipes will serve four people.)

Thai Cuisine

Clear Broth Soup with Coconut, Tofu, and Greens

Yellow Thai Curry with Carrots and Greens

Fresh Cucumber with Basil and Mint

Basmati Rice with Mangoes

Banana Coconut Stew

Clear Broth Soup with Coconut, Tofu, and Greens

1 teaspoon ghee
1 cup (1/4 block) tofu, fresh, low-fat, cut into cubes
2–3 teaspoons Braggs Liquid Amino Acid or tamari sauce
1/4 cup leeks, chopped
1 teaspoon gingerroot, fresh, minced
1/2 teaspoon Chinese five spice
2 cups vegetable stock
1/2 cup carrots, thinly sliced
1/2 cup broccoli, cut into small flowerets
2–3 teaspoons miso, mild flavor
3/4 cup coconut milk, low-fat
1 tightly packed cup spinach greens (baby spinach greens work well)
3 green onions, chopped

In a soup pot, heat the ghee and add the tofu cubes. Brown slightly and add 1 to 2 teaspoons Braggs or tamari sauce. Remove tofu from pot and set aside. Return pot to heat, and add leeks, then add gingerroot and sauté 2 minutes. Add Chinese five spice. Add vegetable stock to the saucepan and bring to a boil. Add sliced carrots and boil for 2 or 3 minutes. Add broccoli, and continue to boil for another 2 minutes. Reduce heat. Using a wire whisk or fork, gently stir in the miso, the remaining 1 teaspoon Braggs, and coconut milk. Check for flavor and add more miso if needed. Divide the spinach greens and the tofu into 4 small bowls. Ladle the broth mixture over the greens and tofu. Garnish with the chopped green onions.

Yellow Thai Curry (mild)

Make the curry paste ahead of time and store in an airtight glass container for up to one month. The secret to a curry paste is dry-roasting the spices.

- 4 stalks lemongrass, fresh (can be found in specialty or Asian markets)
- 2 tablespoons cumin, whole seeds
- 2 tablespoons coriander, whole seeds
- 1 teaspoon red chili flakes
- 1 teaspoon turmeric powder
- 1 teaspoon cinnamon
- 1 teaspoon cardamom
- 1/2 teaspoon asafetida (hing)
- 1/2 cup leeks or onions, finely chopped
- 3 tablespoons ginger, fresh and finely chopped

1 tablespoon Braggs Liquid Amino Acid or tamari sauce
1 teaspoon miso, mild flavor

Begin by trimming the lemongrass stalks. Cut away the grassy tops, leaving about 3 inches of the stalk. Split the root ends and pull away the hard outer sections. The inside root should be smooth and flat. Using a sharp paring knife, cut crosswise into very thin strips. Next, chop into a fine mixture. This process will take a few minutes but will be worth the work. Place the lemongrass in a small bowl.

In a dry heated sauté pan, gently roast the cumin and coriander seeds until just golden brown and the smell is released. Be sure to keep the seeds moving so they don't burn. Add the red chili flakes and roast together for another minute. Place the sautéed chili flakes, cumin, and coriander seeds into a mortar with a pestle or into a spice grinder. Crush or grind into a fine powder. Place into a small mixing bowl and set aside. Add the dry spices to the heated sauté pan and dry-roast for 1 or 2 minutes or until slightly browned. Be sure to move the spices around in the pan to avoid burning. Combine with the roasted spices into the small mixing bowl.

In the heated sauté pan, sauté the leeks and ginger for 3 minutes. Add the Braggs or tamari sauce when the mixture begins to dry out. Add the lemongrass and continue to sauté very briefly, 1 or 2 minutes. Add the leeks and ginger to the bowl of roasted spices. Mix together well. With a teaspoon, begin to work the miso into the mixture. Keep mixing. The curry will break down the more you mix it. Putting some pressure on the spoon will help to pound the spices and leeks together. Add 1/2 teaspoon more miso if needed. If the mixture is too dry and is not combining well, add up to 1 tablespoon vegetable stock. When the mixture is well combined and the consistency of a smooth paste, place into a glass jar and store in the refrigerator. *Note:* You can use a small (mini) food processor to make the paste.

Yellow Thai Curry with Carrots and Greens

Follow the recipe for Yellow Thai Curry. Make a batch, store in a jar with a tight-fitting lid.

1 teaspoon ghee
1 teaspoon sesame oil
1 cup leeks, chopped fine
2 cups carrots, whole, sliced on the diagonal

2 tablespoons vegetable stock
4 tablespoons Yellow Thai Curry paste
4 cups bok choy sliced into long, $1/4$-inch-wide strips
4 cups napa cabbage, thinly sliced
1 tablespoon sesame seeds, toasted
$1/2$ cup cilantro, fresh and chopped
1 tablespoon coconut flakes, toasted
2 limes, juiced

In a large sauté pan, heat up the ghee and sesame oil. Add the leeks and sauté for 2 minutes. Add the carrots and veggie stock and simmer for an additional 2 minutes. Add Thai Curry Paste and simmer for 2 minutes. Add bok choy and napa cabbage. Toss the greens in the curry paste until wilted. Garnish with toasted sesame seeds, chopped cilantro, and coconut; sprinkle with fresh lime juice.

Fresh Cucumber with Basil and Mint

3 cucumbers, peeled, seeds removed, and sliced very thinly
$1/4$ cup, packed, basil, fresh, thinly sliced into strips

- 1/4 cup, packed, mint, fresh, thinly sliced into strips
- 2 tablespoons cilantro, fresh, chopped
- 1/2 teaspoon coriander
- 2 tablespoons rice vinegar
- 1 teaspoon sesame seeds
- 1 teaspoon Braggs Liquid Amino Acid or tamari sauce, *or* 1/2 teaspoon salt

Toss all ingredients together and let rest for up to one hour before serving. Stir a few times while resting to distribute the flavor. Serve as a condiment or side salad.

Basmati Rice with Mangoes

- 2 cups organic basmati rice, rinsed and strained
- 3 3/4 cups water or vegetable stock
- 1 cinnamon stick
- 1/2 cup coconut milk
- 1 cup mango, fresh, ripe, cubed (use defrosted frozen mangoes)
- 1/2 teaspoon cumin
- 1/2 teaspoon cardamom

In a 3-quart saucepan, add the rice and the cinnamon stick to the water or stock and bring to a boil. Cover the pot with a tight-fitting lid and reduce heat. Allow the rice to simmer at the lowest possible heat for 20 minutes. Do not remove the lid from the pot. Remove from heat after 20 minutes. Fluff rice with a fork and add the coconut milk and mango pieces and spices. Fluff with a fork until combined; remove the cinnamon stick before serving. Keep covered until you are ready to serve.

Banana Coconut Stew

1 teaspoon ghee
4 bananas, peeled and sliced
1/2 teaspoon cloves
1/4 cup apple juice
2 tablespoons maple syrup
1/2 cup low-fat coconut milk

In a sauté pan, heat the ghee and add the sliced bananas and simmer for 2 or 3 minutes. Add the cloves and the apple juice. Sauté very briefly, 1 or 2 minutes. Add the maple syrup and the coconut milk. The liquid should just cover the bananas. Add more apple juice to cover the bananas if necessary. Allow the mixture to simmer for 10 minutes. Serve in individual dessert bowls. If desired, garnish with toasted almonds and coconut flakes.

Chinese Cuisine

Vegetable Hot and Sour Soup

Buddha's Feast

Marinated Sesame Tofu Strips

Simple Steamed Rice

Almond Cookies

Vegetable Hot and Sour Soup

1 cup ($^1/_4$ pound) fresh tofu, low-fat, firm or extra firm, cut into thin slices
3 teaspoons Braggs Liquid Amino Acid or tamari sauce
1 teaspoon ghee
1 teaspoon sesame oil
$^1/_2$ teaspoon red chili flakes
1 cup eggplant, peeled and cut into julienne strips

1 cup carrots, thinly sliced
4 cups vegetable stock
2 tablespoons apple cider vinegar
1 tablespoon arrowroot powder
$^{1}/_{4}$ cup cold water
2 tablespoons green onions, chopped
1 cup sunflower sprouts or bean sprouts

Place the tofu into a bowl and add 1 teaspoon of Braggs. Toss with a fork and set aside. In a soup pot heat the ghee and sesame oil. Add chili flakes. Add eggplant and carrots and sauté 3 to 4 minutes or until carrots are almost soft. Add vegetable stock and bring to a boil. Add the tofu, vinegar, and 2 teaspoons Braggs. Simmer 5 minutes. In a small bowl, dissolve the arrowroot in the cold water and combine with a fork. Add to the soup, stirring constantly. The soup will begin to thicken. This only takes a minute. Turn off the heat. Ladle the soup into bowls and garnish with the green onions and sprouts.

Buddha's Feast

Basic Sauce for Chinese Stir-Fry

Yield: 2 cups

3 cloves garlic (optional), pressed, *or* 1 teaspoon powder
1 teaspoon ginger, fresh grated or powder
½ teaspoon red chili flakes
1 tablespoon sesame oil
1½ cups vegetable stock
4 tablespoons Braggs Liquid Amino Acid or tamari sauce
3 tablespoons rice vinegar
1 tablespoon lemon juice
1 tablespoon maple syrup
1 teaspoon mustard, dry
2 tablespoons arrowroot dissolved in 2 tablespoons water

In a small saucepan, lightly sauté the garlic, ginger, and chili flakes in sesame oil. Add all other remaining ingredients except arrowroot and bring just to the boiling point. Reduce the heat and pour in dissolved arrowroot. Stirring continuously, simmer until thickened.

Buddha's Favorite Vegetables

You will need approximately 2 cups of mixed vegetables per person, 8 cups total for 4 servings. Choose any of the following vegetables for a stir-fry. The order given should be the order in which the vegetables will cook.

1 teaspoon ghee
1 teaspoon sesame oil
2 cups carrots, diagonally cut thinly
2 cups carrots, diagonally cut thinly
2 cups cauliflower, bite-size pieces
2 cups broccoli, bite-size pieces, peel stalk and slice
2 cups celery, diagonally cut
2 cups asparagus, 2-inch pieces
2 cups bok choy, sliced diagonally
2 cups cabbage, white or napa, shredded
1 cup red pepper or green pepper, thinly sliced
1 cup green beans, keep whole
2 cups mung bean sprouts
2 cups spinach, shredded
1 cup snow peas, whole

Begin stir-fry by heating 1 teaspoon ghee and 1 teaspoon sesame oil. Reduce this amount if you are making veggies for one or two people.

Adding vegetables one batch at a time according to the order, stir-fry until the carrots are tender. Pour sauce over vegetables after they are cooked. Serve over rice or udon noodles. Garnish with sesame seeds and green onions.

Marinade Sesame Tofu Strips

12 ounces fresh tofu, low-fat, firm, or extra firm, cut into cubes or slices
$^1/_4$ cup sesame seeds, toasted

Marinade

$^1/_2$ cup rice vinegar
$^1/_2$ cup Braggs Liquid Amino Acid or tamari sauce
2 tablespoons maple syrup
2 tablespoons lemon juice
1 teaspoon cumin, ground
1 teaspoon ginger, ground
1 teaspoon sesame oil

Combine the marinade ingredients. Cut tofu into desired shape and soak in marinade for 6 hours or overnight. Remove the tofu from the marinade. Place sesame seeds in a small bowl and coat each the piece of tofu with sesame seeds. Place tofu on a sheet pan sprayed with oil. Bake in the oven until the tofu is golden brown, 20 to 30 minutes. Add to the stir-fry or use in any dish that calls for tofu cubes.

Simple Steamed Rice

1 cup basmati rice
2 cups water or vegetable stock

Bring rice and water to a boil. Reduce heat to lowest possible setting and allow the rice to cook undisturbed for 15 to 20 minutes. Fluff with a fork and serve with stir-fry.

Almond Cookies

1 cup almonds (you can use any type of nut)
1 cup rolled oats, organic

Place the almonds in a food processor and pulse for 1 minute. Add the oats and continue to pulse into a coarse meal. Place mixture into a mixing bowl.

1 cup whole wheat pastry flour or rice flour
$^1/_2$ teaspoon cinnamon or nutmeg
$^1/_2$ teaspoon salt
$^1/_2$ cup maple syrup
$^1/_4$ cup canola oil or ghee
$^1/_4$ cup mango puree or applesauce or mashed banana
12–15 almonds, whole

Place the flour, almond/oat mixture, cinnamon, and salt into the mixing bowl. Mix together with a wire whisk. In a separate bowl, combine the maple syrup, oil, and mango (or fruit puree) together and mix with a wire whisk. Combine the wet and the dry ingredients with your hands (use plastic bags on your hands). Mix into a smooth consistency. Using a small 1-ounce scoop or a tablespoon, scoop mixture onto a sprayed baking sheet. Make a small dip with your thumb and place a whole almond into the center of the cookie. Bake at 350 degrees 20 to 25 minutes or until golden brown.

Italian Cuisine

White Bean and Vegetable Soup

Spinach and Eggplant Layered Pasta with Pesto

Roasted Tomato Sauce

Garbanzo and Green Bean Stew

Roasted Carrots with Fresh Rosemary

Raspberry Tofu Sorbet

White Bean and Vegetable Soup

1 cup white beans, soak in water overnight, strain and rinse in the morning

Place the beans in a soup pot. Fill the pot with water to a level that is 2 inches above the beans. Bring to a boil. Allow the beans to cook until soft, but not mushy. Replenish the water as needed to maintain a rolling boil. Strain the beans and reserve. Discard the liquid.

1 teaspoon ghee or olive oil
1 cup leeks, chopped

Sauté together 2 minutes, and then add, in order:

1 cup celery
½ teaspoon black pepper
1 teaspoon basil

1 teaspoon marjoram
1 teaspoon dill
1 teaspoon oregano
1 tablespoon Braggs Liquid Amino Acid
1 cup carrots, $^{1}/_{4}$-inch slices
1 cup cauliflower, cut into flowerets

Sauté together 5 minutes, stirring frequently. Next add:

1 cup zucchini
2 cups white beans, cooked
5–6 cups vegetable stock (enough to cover, plus one inch)
2 bay leaves

Simmer together until the vegetables are tender, approximately 20 minutes.

1 cup, packed, mixed cooking greens or spinach
2 tablespoons organic tomato paste
1 tablespoon basil, fresh, sliced thinly
1 tablespoon parsley, fresh, chopped

Add the mixed greens, tomato paste, and fresh herbs toward the end. Stir until the paste begins to thicken. Serve in large soup bowls.

Spinach and Eggplant Layered Pasta with Pesto

Pesto

2 cups, packed, fresh basil, stems removed
1 cup broccoli, coarsely chopped and lightly sautéed in 1 teaspoon olive oil
½ cup pine nuts (dry-roasted in a sauté pan until golden brown)
2 tablespoons lemon juice
3 tablespoons olive oil
½ teaspoon Braggs Liquid Amino Acid or salt

In a food processor, place the basil and sautéed broccoli and pulse for 1 minute. Add the pine nuts, lemon juice, oil, and Braggs. Puree until a smooth consistency is achieved.

Pasta

9 fresh or dried 2 × 9-inch strips pasta

Use fresh pasta sheets if available or dry lasagna noodles. Cut fresh sheet into 2-inch strips. Use the dry lasagna sheets as they are. Bring 3 quarts of water to a boil in a large pot. Dip the noodles in the boiling water and cook until tender. Boil the fresh pasta 2 to 3 minutes, the dry pasta 6 to 7 minutes. Remove from cooking water and set aside in fresh cool water until ready to use. Drain just before you assemble the casserole.

Filling

1 tablespoon Italian herb
2 teaspoons black pepper
1 tablespoon olive oil
1 tablespoon Braggs Liquid Amino Acid
1 large or 2 medium eggplant, sliced in $\frac{1}{4}$-inch rounds (approx. 18 slices), discard ends
2 pounds fresh spinach, cleaned and torn into pieces, blanched for 2 minutes in boiling water, rinsed in cool water and set aside, *or* two 10-ounce packages frozen spinach, defrosted
1 teaspoon dill, dried
1 teaspoon allspice
$\frac{1}{2}$ teaspoon paprika
$\frac{1}{4}$ cup bread crumbs

Combine the Italian herb, 1 teaspoon pepper, oil, and Braggs. Place eggplant into a large bowl and drizzle the olive oil mixture on top. Toss the eggplant until well coated. On a sheet pan, lay out the eggplant and roast in the oven for 20 minutes, or until the eggplant is almost tender. Remove from the oven and cool. Place the spinach in a bowl and add the dill, allspice, and remaining teaspoon of black pepper. In a separate bowl, mix the paprika and bread crumbs together with your hands (use plastic bags on your hands for cleanliness) and set aside.

To Assemble:

Spray an 8 × 8-inch-square casserole pan with olive oil or coat lightly with ghee. On the bottom of the pan lay down three strips of pasta. Layer half of the eggplant on top of the pasta. Spread half the pesto on top of the eggplant. Layer half of the spinach on top of the pesto; if desired, add grated cheese. Place another 3 strips of pasta on top and press into the pan with your fingers. Layer the rest of the eggplant, pesto, and spinach in the same way. Place the remaining pasta on top of the spinach, pressing it together with your fingertips. Brush olive oil or ghee lightly on top of the casserole, sprinkle with paprika and bread crumbs. Cover with parchment paper and foil. Place in the oven at 350 degrees and bake for 30 minutes. Serve with Roasted Tomato Sauce.

Roasted Tomato Sauce

Makes one quart

12 small tomatoes, washed and with a small "X" cut into the top of each; cut off the ends
$^1/_4$ cup olive oil
1 teaspoon black pepper
4 sprigs rosemary, fresh, removed from stem
1 tablespoon basil, dried
1 teaspoon thyme, dried
1 tablespoon balsamic vinegar

To roast tomatoes: In a bowl, toss the tomatoes with the other ingredients, then place in a shallow roasting pan. Bake at 350 degrees for 20 to 30 minutes, or until the tomatoes are soft and the skin is easily removed. Allow to cool, then remove and discard skin. By hand, break up the tomatoes and discard the seeds. Place the tomatoes into a strainer set inside a bowl to collect the juice. Set aside, allowing the tomatoes to drain.

1 tablespoon ghee or olive oil
1/2 teaspoon red chili flakes
1 teaspoon black pepper
2 cups leeks or shallots, chopped

Place ghee and spices into a heated 4-quart saucepan; add leeks and sauté until they are soft. Add tomatoes and simmer at least 30 minutes or up to an hour on a very low heat. Add the following except the parley and basil, during simmering.

1/2 cup roasted red pepper, fresh or canned, drained and chopped
1 teaspoon balsamic vinegar
1/4 cup parsley, fresh, chopped
1/2 cup basil, fresh, thinly sliced

Remove from heat, add parsley and basil and puree with a hand blender.

Garbanzo and Green Bean Stew

1 cup garbanzo beans or chickpeas, covered with water and soaked overnight

Place the beans in a soup pot. Fill the pot with water to a level that is 2 inches above the beans. Bring to a boil. Allow the beans to cook until soft but not mushy. Replenish the water as needed to maintain a rolling boil. Strain the beans and set aside. Discard the liquid.

1 teaspoon ghee or olive oil
1 cup leeks, chopped
1 teaspoon black pepper
1 teaspoon Braggs Liquid Amino Acid or tamari sauce
2 cups, packed, fresh green beans, stems removed, cut into 1-inch pieces
1 teaspoon basil, dried
1 teaspoon dill, dried
1 teaspoon oregano
½ cup vegetable stock
1½ cups fresh tomatoes, diced or organic diced canned tomatoes
2 cups cooked garbanzo beans

In a sauté pan, heat the ghee or olive oil and add the leeks. Add the pepper and the Braggs. Simmer for 2 minutes. Next, add the green beans and spices. Add $^{1}/_{4}$ cup of vegetable stock and simmer for 3 to 4 minutes. Add the tomatoes, garbanzos, and the rest of the vegetable stock. Simmer until the green beans are tender. Most of the liquid will be absorbed.

Roasted Carrots with Fresh Rosemary

1 teaspoon ghee or olive oil
1 teaspoon curry powder
1 teaspoon dill, dried
1 teaspoon nutmeg
1 tablespoon fresh rosemary leaves, removed from stem and coarsely chopped
1 teaspoon Braggs Liquid Amino Acid or tamari sauce
6 large carrots, peeled and cut into 1-inch cubes

Whisk together everything except the carrots in a large mixing bowl. Add the carrots and toss with your hands until well coated. On a sprayed sheet pan, lay out the carrots and roast in a 350-degree oven. Roast until tender, about 20 minutes.

Raspberry Tofu Sorbet

One 10-ounce bag raspberries, frozen (organic)
One 10-ounce bag strawberries, frozen (organic)
One 12-ounce container Mori Nu or silken tofu, low-fat, firm or extra firm
$^1/_4$ cup maple syrup
1 teaspoon vanilla extract
$^1/_4$ teaspoon cloves
Toasted coconut flakes
Toasted sliced almonds

In a food processor, pulse berries until almost smooth. Add tofu and continue to puree; add maple syrup, vanilla, and cloves. Continue to puree until a smooth texture is achieved. Remove from the food processor and scoop out into bowls. Garnish with toasted coconut flakes and toasted sliced almonds. Store any leftovers in the freezer.

MEXICAN CUISINE

Tortilla Soup with Avocado and Cilantro

Black Bean and Sweet Potato Enchiladas

Spanish Rice

Mango and Tomato Salsa

Baked Vanilla Flan with Maple Syrup

Tortilla Soup with Avocado and Cilantro

2 teaspoons ghee
1 cup leeks, chopped
1 teaspoon Braggs Liquid Amino Acid or tamari sauce
1 teaspoon black pepper
1/2 teaspoon red chili flakes
1 teaspoon chili powder (mild)
1 teaspoon cumin
1 cup carrots, cut into bite-size pieces
1/2 cup green bell pepper, chopped
4 cups vegetable stock
1 cup corn, fresh or frozen (organic)
1/4 cup roasted pepper, fresh or from a jar, chopped

2 corn tortillas, cut into 1-inch-thick strips
1 cup fresh avocado, cubed
1/4 cup, packed, cilantro, chopped
Several sprigs cilantro with stems
(for garnish)

In a soup pot, heat 1 teaspoon of the ghee and add the leeks. Add the Braggs, pepper, and other spices. Sauté for 1 minute. Next, add the carrots and bell pepper. Sauté for 2 minutes and then add 1/2 cup vegetable stock. Continue to simmer 4 to 5 minutes. Add the corn, roasted pepper, and the rest of the stock. Allow the soup to simmer until the carrots are almost soft. In a small sauté pan, heat the remaining 1 teaspoon of ghee and add the tortillas. Quickly stir-fry the tortillas until they become crisp. Remove from heat and stir the tortillas into the soup along with the chopped cilantro. Divide the avocado among individual bowls. Ladle the soup over the avocado and garnish with the cilantro sprigs. Serve right away.

Black Bean and Sweet Potato Enchiladas

1 cup black beans, soaked overnight, or one 12-ounce can organic black beans
2 cups sweet potato, peeled and cubed into small pieces
1 teaspoon ghee
1 cup leeks, chopped
1 teaspoon black pepper
½ teaspoon red chili flakes
1 tablespoon Braggs Liquid Amino Acid or tamari sauce
1 cup spinach or chard, chopped
½ teaspoon cinnamon
1 teaspoon oregano
1 teaspoon cumin
Vegetable stock
¼ cup cilantro, stems removed and chopped

If you are using dried black beans, place the beans in a 3- or 4-quart pot, fill with water to a least 3 inches above the beans. Allow the black beans to cook until tender, about 1 hour. Replenish the water as necessary. Drain the beans from the pot when they become tender. Bring a 2-quart pot of water to a boil, add sweet potatoes and boil for 5 minutes. The potatoes will be almost soft. Drain potatoes and set aside.

In a sauté pan, heat the ghee and add the leeks, add pepper, chili flakes, and Braggs. Allow the leeks to simmer 2 to 3 minutes. Reduce heat and add the cooked black beans and cooked sweet potatoes. Continue to simmer on low heat. Add some vegetable stock if the mixture becomes too dry.

Add the greens to the mixture as it continues to simmer. Add the remaining spices. With a fork, gently mash the ingredients together as they simmer. Stir in the cilantro and remove from the heat. Set aside.

Enchilada Sauce

You can purchase a good-quality organic enchilada sauce at the health food store or make the following recipe.

1 teaspoon ghee
1 cup leeks or onions
1 teaspoon black pepper
1 teaspoon Braggs Liquid Amino Acid or tamari sauce
3 cups or 5 medium-size tomatoes, chopped (peeling and seeding optional)
1 teaspoon cumin
1 teaspoon coriander
2 teaspoons chili powder

1 cup tomato juice or vegetable stock
1 package of 12 corn tortillas

Heat the ghee in a sauté pan; add the leeks or onions, pepper, and Braggs. Allow the leeks to simmer 2 to 3 minutes. As the leeks begin to brown slightly, add the tomatoes and the rest of the spices. Slowly add the juice and continue to simmer for 20 to 30 minutes allowing the juices to reduce. Puree in a blender or use a hand blender. This sauce should be smooth and a little bit thick. Heat the tortillas in a sauté pan one at a time. Place some of the sauce in a shallow pan and dip the heated tortilla on both sides into the sauce. Transfer into a sprayed baking pan. Fill the heated tortilla with the filling and roll over, tucking in each side. Repeat this procedure for each of the tortillas you want to fill. Pour the remaining sauce over the rolled tortillas and bake covered at 350 degrees for 20 to 30 minutes. You can add dairy or soy cheese on top if you want. Garnish with freshly chopped cilantro.

Spanish Rice

1 cup basmati rice, organic, rinsed
2 cups plus 1 tablespoon vegetable stock

1 teaspoon ghee
½ cup leeks or onions
½ teaspoon black pepper
1 teaspoon Braggs Liquid Amino Acid or tamari sauce
1 teaspoon paprika
1 teaspoon chili powder
1 teaspoon cumin
½ cup corn, fresh or organic, frozen and defrosted
½ cup peas, fresh or organic, frozen and defrosted

Combine the rice and 2 cups stock and cook in a rice cooker or on the stove until tender. In a separate sauté pan, heat the ghee. Add the leeks, pepper, and Braggs, allowing the leeks to brown slightly. Add the remaining spices, corn, peas, and tablespoon of vegetable stock. Simmer for 1 minute. Stir the paprika mixture into the cooked rice.

Mango and Tomato Salsa

1 cup fresh mango or papaya, cubed
$^1/_4$ cup orange or apple juice
$^1/_4$ cup cilantro, chopped and loosely packed
$^1/_4$ cup leeks or green onions, chopped (sauté leeks slightly first)
1 tablespoon lemon juice
1 tablespoon maple syrup
1 teaspoon coriander
$^1/_2$ teaspoon allspice
$^1/_2$ teaspoon cinnamon
$^1/_2$ teaspoon nutmeg
$^1/_2$ teaspoon cardamom, ground
$^1/_4$ teaspoon crushed red pepper (cayenne)

Combine together, chill, and serve.

Baked Vanilla Flan with Maple Syrup

12 ounces silken tofu, low-fat, firm, or extra firm
$^1/_4$ cup maple syrup
2 teaspoons vanilla extract
2 teaspoons arrowroot powder

pinch cloves
6 teaspoons raw turbinado sugar
6 teaspoons maple syrup

With a blender or food processor blend the first five ingredients together until smooth. Spray or butter 6 baking dishes. Divide the tofu mixture into the 6 dishes. Bake at 350 degrees for 15 minutes. Remove from the oven and sprinkle 1 teaspoon of sugar and pour 1 teaspoon of maple syrup onto the top of each dessert dish. Place back into the oven for 5 minutes or until the tops are golden brown. Serve warm.

French Cuisine

Creamy Asparagus Soup

Spinach, Leek, and Potato Tart

Braised Green Beans Amandine

Swiss Chard and Arugula with Lemon Tarragon Dressing

Poached Pears with Blackberries

Creamy Asparagus Soup

2 teaspoons ghee
2 large leeks, chopped
1 teaspoon black pepper
1 teaspoon Braggs Liquid Amino Acid or tamari sauce
$\frac{1}{4}$ pound white potatoes, peeled and cubed
1 tablespoon tarragon
1 teaspoon thyme
$\frac{3}{4}$ pound asparagus, discard bottom $1\frac{1}{2}$ inch and cut into 1-inch pieces
4–6 cups vegetable stock or to cover potatoes in pot
$\frac{1}{2}$ teaspoon nutmeg
2 tablespoons parsley, chopped

In a large soup pot, heat the ghee. Sauté the leeks and add pepper and Braggs. Continue to simmer the leeks. Add the potatoes, tarragon, and thyme. Sauté until the potatoes are browned. Add the asparagus pieces and cover the vegetables with vegetable stock. Simmer until the potatoes are tender. Puree the soup into a smooth consistency by using either a handheld blender, standard blender, or food processor. Garnish soup with nutmeg and parsley.

Spinach, Leek, and Potato Tart

Crust

- $1\frac{1}{2}$ cups organic unbleached white flour or whole wheat pastry flour
- $\frac{1}{2}$ teaspoon salt
- $\frac{1}{2}$ cup butter (or soy margarine), chilled and cut into pieces
- 1 teaspoon lemon juice or vinegar
- $\frac{1}{4}$ cup water, chilled

Place the "S" blade in the food processor. Put the flour and salt in the bottom of the processor. Turn on the machine and begin to drop the butter pieces into the flour mixture, a few at a time. Once all the butter is in the food processor, switch to "pulse" and pulse the dough until the mixture resembles a coarse meal. Add the lemon juice and pulse 3 to 4 times. Turn the food processor to "on" and slowly drizzle the water into the mixture until stiff dough begins to form.

Turn the dough out onto a floured countertop. Bring the dough together with your hands and form into a flat, round disk. Roll out the dough evenly, using a rolling pin. Gently place the rolled dough into a sprayed 9- or 10-inch tart pan. Using your fingers, begin to press the dough toward the outer edges and create a $1/2$-inch edge along the wall of the tart pan. Place the tart in the refrigerator until you are ready to assemble.

Filling

- 2 teaspoons ghee or olive oil
- 4 medium-size red potatoes, sliced very thinly in rounds
- 2 large leeks, sliced thinly in rounds
- 1 teaspoon black pepper
- 1 teaspoon basil, dried
- 1 teaspoon sage, dried
- 2 teaspoons Braggs Liquid Amino Acid or tamari sauce
- 4 packed cups spinach, organic, *or* one 10-ounce package frozen, defrosted and chopped
- 1 teaspoon dill, dried
- 1 teaspoon marjoram, dried
- One 10-ounce package silken tofu, low-fat, firm or extra firm

$^1/_4$–$^1/_2$ cup vegetable stock
1 tablespoon arrowroot dissolved in
  1 tablespoon water

In a large sauté pan, heat 1 teaspoon of ghee. Lightly sauté potatoes until just browned on both sides. Remove from the pan and set aside. Heat another teaspoon of ghee in the sauté pan and put the leeks, pepper, basil, sage, and 1 teaspoon Braggs into sauté. Try to keep the leeks in rings. Sauté until golden brown. Remove from pan and set aside. If you are using fresh spinach, heat the sauté pan again and briefly sauté the spinach until wilted. Remove from the heat. In a mixing bowl, place the cooked or defrosted spinach. Add the herbs and toss together. In a blender, begin to blend the tofu, adding the stock slowly as the tofu becomes smooth. Add the arrowroot that has been dissolved and the remaining teaspoon of Braggs. Blend until a light, smooth consistency is achieved. If the mixture is too thick, add a little more stock. Add $^1/_2$ cup of the tofu mix to the spinach. Mix together well.

To assemble: Place the sautéed leeks on the bottom of the refrigerated tart pan, spread a layer of the spinach mixture on top of the leeks. Pour the tofu mixture on top of the spinach. This layer should just cover the spinach and be about 1/4 inch thick. Reserve any extra for another use. Arrange the potatoes on top of the casserole in a circular or rectangular design. Sprinkle paprika, dill, and nutmeg on top of the tart for color. Bake at 350 degrees for 35 minutes or until an inserted knife comes out clean from the middle of the tart and the potatoes are golden brown.

Braised Green Beans Amandine

1 teaspoon ghee
2 large handfuls green beans, fresh and organic
1 teaspoon cumin
1 teaspoon balsamic vinegar
1/4 cup almonds, sliced and toasted in the oven
vegetable stock

In a sauté pan, heat the ghee and add the green beans. Add the cumin and continue to simmer. If the beans get too dry add 1 teaspoon of vegetable stock. Simmer until the green beans are almost tender. Just before serving add the balsamic vinegar. Toss the green beans around in the pan to coat with the vinegar. Sprinkle the almonds on top of the individual portion or in the serving bowl.

Swiss Chard and Arugula with Lemon Tarragon Dressing

1 bunch red swiss chard, washed
1 cup arugula, cleaned and stems removed
$^1/_4$ cup vegetable stock
2 tablespoons Lemon Tarragon Dressing

Heat a dry sauté pan and add the chard and the arugula. Allow the greens to wilt. Only add stock to the pan if it is too hot and the greens begin to brown. Toss the finished greens with the Lemon Tarragon Dressing.

Lemon Tarragon Dressing

$^1/_4$ cup parsley, chopped
1 green onion, chopped
$^1/_4$ cup lemon juice
1 teaspoon Dijon mustard
1 tablespoon tarragon

2 tablespoons maple syrup
1 teaspoon Braggs Liquid Amino Acid
1/4 cup apple juice
1/4 cup olive oil

Combine everything but oil in a blender. Slowly add the oil as the blender continues to run. Continue to blend until the dressing begins to thicken slightly.

Poached Pears with Blackberries

1 can apple juice concentrate, organic
2 Bosc or D'Anjou pears, cut in half, peeled, and cored
1/2 teaspoon cloves, whole
2 cinnamon sticks
1 tablespoon lemon juice
2 tablespoons cranberries, dried
One 10-ounce package blackberries, frozen and organic, *or* 1 box, fresh in season
1–2 tablespoons maple syrup
Cinnamon or nutmeg for garnish

Heat the apple juice concentrate in a sauté pan. Add the pears, cloves, cinnamon sticks, lemon juice, and the cranberries. Allow the pears to simmer in the juice until the pears are tender. If the liquid is absorbed and the pears become uncovered, add more apple juice or water. The pears need to remain submerged. In a separate heated sauté pan, place the blackberries and begin to sauté. Reduce heat and allow the blackberries to break down and create juice. Add a little apple juice if needed to create some liquid. Add the maple syrup just before serving. Adjust the amount by the tartness or the sweetness of the berries. To serve: Remove the pears from the liquid (reserve the liquid for another use). Place a pear in the middle of a dessert plate. Spoon on the berries and some of the juice from the berry sauté. To garnish, sprinkle with cinnamon or nutmeg.

American Bistro Cuisine

Carrot Coriander Soup

Roasted Vegetable Barley Risotto

Cranberry and Sweet Potato Chutney

Organic Field Greens with Apple Vinaigrette

Cocoa Tofu Mousse with Almond Praline

Carrot Coriander Soup

1 teaspoon ghee
1 cup leeks, chopped
1 tablespoon ginger, fresh, chopped
1 teaspoon black pepper
½ teaspoon red chili flakes
1 tablespoon Braggs Liquid Amino Acid or tamari sauce
3 cups carrots, cubed
¼ cup golden raisins, chopped
2 teaspoons coriander, dried
1 teaspoon cumin
1 teaspoon asafetida
4–5 cups vegetable stock
1 teaspoon lemon juice
1 cup low-fat coconut milk
2 tablespoons cilantro or parsley

In a soup pot, heat up the ghee and add the leeks and the ginger. Add the pepper, chili flakes, and 1 teaspoon of Braggs. Add the carrots and the raisins. Sauté for 2 to 3 minutes. Add the coriander, cumin, asafetida and the rest of the Braggs. Continue to sauté 3 to 5 minutes. Sauté until lightly browned. If the mixture gets too dry, add a little broth. Add vegetable stock to cover and bring to a boil. Cook the soup until carrots are soft. Puree soup with a food processor or a hand blender. Add lemon and coconut milk just before serving. Garnish with freshly chopped cilantro or parsley.

Roasted Vegetable Barley Risotto

Barley

1 teaspoon ghee or olive oil
3 medium-size leeks, chopped
6–8 cups vegetable stock, made flavorful by adding herbs and leeks
1 teaspoon Braggs Liquid Amino Acid or tamari sauce
1 teaspoon balsamic vinegar
1 tablespoon basil, dried
1 teaspoon black pepper
2 cups pearl barley, organic

In a heated braising pan, heat ghee and add the leeks. Sauté 1 minute, add 2 tablespoons vegetable stock, Braggs, vinegar, basil, and pepper. Sauté until the leeks are clear. Add the barley. With a large spoon, toss the barley around in the pan to brown. Don't let the barley get too dry. Add $1/2$ cup of stock, if necessary. Sauté until the barley becomes golden brown or caramelized. Continue to add $^1/_2$ cup of stock at a time when the mixture becomes dry. Always add enough stock to cover the barley as it cooks. Keep a lid handy to use during the cooking process. Continue to check and stir the barley every few minutes to make sure enough liquid is in the pot to cover the barley. This will take up to 30 minutes at a rapid boil.

Roasted Vegetables

2 carrots
2 zucchini
1 medium-size eggplant
1 tablespoon olive oil
1 tablespoon Braggs Liquid Amino Acid or tamari sauce
1 tablespoon balsamic vinegar
1 teaspoon black pepper
1 tablespoon Italian herbs

Remove the ends from the carrots, zucchini, and eggplant. Cut each in half. Slice each into $^1/_4$-inch slices. Set aside. Combine the oil, Braggs, vinegar, pepper, and Italian herbs in a large bowl. Whisk together with a wire whisk. Add the vegetables and coat with the marinade. Remove from the bowl and lay out on a sprayed sheet pan. Roast in the oven for 30 minutes at

350 degrees. You can also cook them on an outside grill. Remove from oven and cool off.

To Assemble

- ½ cup roasted red pepper, fresh or from a jar
- 1 cup white beans, cooked, *or* 1 can, rinsed
- 1 tablespoon fresh rosemary, chopped
- 1 tablespoon fresh mint, chopped
- 2 tablespoons fresh basil, thinly sliced
- 1 cup tomatoes, chopped
- ¼ cup parsley, chopped

As the barley continues to cook, and the liquid absorbs, keep adding the stock until the barley is tender to the taste. Be careful not to overcook. Slice your roasted vegetables into 1-inch bite-size pieces. Add the chopped vegetables into the pot with the cooked barley. Add the roasted red peppers and the cooked white beans. Add freshly chopped rosemary, mint, and basil to the pot. Toss all ingredients. Place the risotto into an attractive serving dish and garnish with freshly chopped parsley and tomatoes. Add your favorite grated cheese for a rich taste.

Cranberry and Sweet Potato Chutney

1 teaspoon ghee
½ cup leeks or shallots, chopped
1 teaspoon black pepper
1 teaspoon Braggs Liquid Amino Acid or tamari sauce
2 cups sweet potato, diced into small pieces
1 cup cranberries, dried
1 can apple juice concentrate, organic, frozen
½ teaspoon cloves, whole
3 cinnamon sticks
½ teaspoon cardamom, dried
1 tablespoon balsamic vinegar
1 teaspoon apple cider vinegar
½ teaspoon coriander

In a sauté pan heat the ghee and add leeks. Sauté for 1 minute and then add pepper, Braggs, and the sweet potatoes. Sauté together for 3 to 4 minutes. Add the cranberries and apple juice. As the apple juice concentrate begins to melt, add the cloves and the cinnamon sticks. Add the cardamom, balsamic vinegar, apple cider vinegar, and the coriander once the liquid is melted and a rolling simmer is achieved. Allow the mixture to simmer at a reduced heat for up to an hour. The liquid should reduce to create a smooth yet thick consistency. Serve warm or chilled.

Organic Field Greens with Apple Vinaigrette

1 large Granny Smith apple, chopped
1 tablespoon lemon juice poured into $^1/_2$ cup water
$^1/_4$ cup almonds, roasted
3 cups organic field greens
1 cup spinach, washed
$^1/_4$ cup feta cheese, crumbled
$^1/_2$ cup cherry tomatoes or yellow pear tomatoes
1 cup sunflower or alfalfa sprouts

Dressing

1 cup apple juice
$^1/_4$ cup balsamic vinegar
$^1/_4$ cup honey
1 teaspoon tarragon
1 teaspoon thyme
2 tablespoons parsley, chopped
2 tablespoons basil, chopped
$^1/_4$ cup olive oil

Soak the chopped apples in the lemon water.

Place the almonds on a baking sheet and roast in the oven for 20 minutes or briefly dry sauté them.

Combine the dressing ingredients in a blender minus the olive oil. Blend until smooth. Slowly add the olive oil and blend until the mixture begins to thicken.

Place the greens, drained apples, feta cheese, and tomatoes in a salad bowl. Toss with the dressing. Arrange the salad on a plate and garnish with almonds and sunflower sprouts.

Cocoa Tofu Mousse with Almond Praline

2 tablespoons ghee, unsalted butter, or canola oil (for a vegan dessert)
2 tablespoons apple juice
1 cup Semi Sweet Chocolate Chips (Tropical Source)
2 teaspoons vanilla extract
12 ounces silken tofu, low-fat, firm or extra firm
1/4 cup maple syrup
2 teaspoons vanilla extract
Coconut or fresh fruit for garnish

In a small saucepan, melt the ghee and apple juice with the chips and vanilla. Stir frequently to avoid burning. Use a double boiler if you like. When the chips are melted, remove from the heat and stir into a creamy consistency. Set aside.

In a blender or food processor, combine tofu, syrup, and vanilla extract. Blend at high speed for one minute. Scrape the sides down and continue to blend into a smooth consistency. Add the melted chips to the blender or processor. Continue to blend until smooth and well incorporated. Spoon the mousse into small dessert bowls or reserve in a container with a tight-fitting lid. Place in the refrigerator to chill.

Almond Praline

1 tablespoon ghee
2 tablespoons maple syrup
1 cup almonds, sliced

Heat the ghee and maple syrup in a small sauté pan. Add the almonds. Stirring frequently, coat the almonds well and sauté until golden brown. Remove from heat and cool off. Garnish mousse with almond praline and coconut or fresh fruit.

Middle Eastern Cuisine

Spinach and Lentil Soup

Hummus

Quinoa Tabouli

Creamy Tofu Cucumber and Mint Raita

Ratatouille Stew

Maple Walnut Filo Triangles

Spinach and Lentil Soup

1 teaspoon ghee
½ teaspoon red chili flakes
3 cloves garlic (optional)
1 teaspoon ginger
2 cups leeks or onions
½ teaspoon black pepper
1 teaspoon rosemary, fresh, chopped
1 tablespoon Braggs Liquid Amino Acid or
  tamari sauce
½ cup bulgur wheat
1 teaspoon cumin
½ teaspoon allspice
1 cup lentils, sorted and rinsed

5 cups vegetable stock
2 bay leaves
2 tablespoons tomato paste
4 cups fresh spinach, chopped

In a soup pot, heat the ghee and add the red chili flakes, garlic, ginger, and leeks. Add pepper, rosemary, and Braggs. Sauté for 2 to 3 minutes. Add the bulgur and sauté until golden brown. Add the cumin and allspice and continue to sauté. Add the rinsed lentils, the stock, and the bay leaves. Bring the soup to a boil. Add tomato paste and then reduce the heat. Allow the soup to simmer at a soft rolling boil until the lentils are soft. Add the spinach and allow to wilt. Divide into soup bowls with the following garnish.

Garnish

$\frac{1}{4}$ cup parsley, freshly chopped
2 cups tomatoes, chopped
2 cloves garlic, fresh, minced (optional)

Combine the parsley, tomatoes, and optional garlic and place into individual bowls. Ladle the soup over the mixture.

Hummus

$^{1}/_{4}$ cup parsley, chopped
1 large green onion, chopped, *or*
1 tablespoon leek, chopped
2 teaspoons minced garlic, *or*
1 teaspoon garlic powder
1 cup garbanzo beans soaked overnight and cooked until tender
2 tablespoons tahini
2 tablespoons lemon juice
2 teaspoons Braggs Liquid Amino Acid or tamari sauce
1 teaspoon cumin
$^{1}/_{4}$ teaspoon cayenne
1 teaspoon dill, dried

Place parsley, green onion, and garlic in a food processor. Use "Pulse" to chop. Add the remaining ingredients and process until smooth. Taste and adjust lemon juice and/or spices to taste. Hummus should have a loose consistency but hold together when in a dollop.

Quinoa Tabouli

1 cup quinoa
2 cups boiling water
1 teaspoon ghee or olive oil
½ cup leeks or onions, chopped
¼ cup vegetable stock
2 cups tomatoes, diced, or any combination of vegetables cut into small cubes (zucchini, squash, carrots, sweet potato)
1 cup garbanzo beans, or white beans, cooked
½ cup Italian parsley, fresh, chopped
¼ cup mint, fresh, chopped
2 tablespoons Kalamata olives, chopped, pits removed

Dressing

¼ cup lemon juice
1 tablespoon olive oil
1 tablespoon balsamic vinegar
1 teaspoon dill, dried
½ teaspoon each salt and black pepper
2 cloves garlic, pressed, *or* 1 teaspoon garlic powder

Bring 2 cups of water to a boil. Add the quinoa and cover with a lid. Reduce the heat and allow to simmer for 15 to 20 minutes, or until the liquid is absorbed. Fluff with a fork and place into mixing bowl and set aside. Heat sauté pan with ghee or olive oil. Add leeks and sauté briefly. Add vegetable stock as the mixture begins to dry out. Add 2 cups of vegetables and sauté until lightly browned. Keep the tomatoes fresh. You don't need to sauté them. Remove the vegetables from the heat and cool off. Combine beans, parsley, mint, and olives in the bowl with the quinoa. Toss with hands to combine well (use plastic bags over your hands). In a separate bowl, whisk together the dressing ingredients and pour over the quinoa mixture. This pilaf can be served hot with an entrée or used as a stuffing for vegetables such as artichokes, zucchini, squash. It also makes a great cold salad.

Creamy Tofu Cucumber and Mint Raita

6 ounces silken tofu, low-fat, firm or extra firm
1/4 cup lemon juice
1 teaspoon Braggs Liquid Amino Acid or tamari sauce
1 teaspoon cumin

1 teaspoon dill, dried
2 cucumbers, seeded, peeled, and chopped
$\frac{1}{2}$ packed cup mint, freshly chopped
$\frac{1}{4}$ packed cup cilantro, freshly chopped

In a blender or food processor place the tofu, lemon juice, and Braggs. Blend until smooth. Add the cumin and dill. Remove from the blender and place mixture into a bowl. Add the chopped cucumber and fresh herbs. If the mixture is too thick, add some apple juice or water to bring it up to a creamy consistency. You can also use yogurt in place of the tofu.

Ratatouille Stew

1 tablespoon olive oil or ghee
2 large leeks, chopped
1 teaspoon black pepper
1 teaspoon garlic powder (optional)
1 tablespoon Braggs Liquid Amino Acid
2 teaspoons Italian spices
1 large eggplant, diced
2 large zucchinis, cubed
3 large bell peppers, green and red, cubed

2 cups tomatoes, diced
$1\frac{1}{2}$ cups vegetable stock
$\frac{1}{2}$ cup basil, sliced thinly

In a large soup pot, heat the olive oil and then add the leeks, pepper, garlic, Braggs, and Italian spices. Add the eggplant, zucchini, and bell peppers and sauté for 4 to 5 minutes. Add the tomatoes and continue to simmer. Add the vegetable stock when the mixture begins to dry out. The stew should simmer for 20 to 30 minutes at a low heat. Add the fresh basil just before serving.

Maple Filo Walnut Triangles

1 teaspoon ghee
2 tablespoons maple syrup
2 cups walnuts, chopped coarsely
$\frac{1}{4}$ cup coconut flakes
1 teaspoon cinnamon
12 sheets whole wheat pastry filo
$\frac{1}{4}$ cup ghee or vegetable spray
1 teaspoon nutmeg

Heat the ghee and maple syrup in a sauté pan. Add the walnuts and sauté until well coated. Stir in the coconut flakes and cinnamon. Continue to combine until well coated.

Cut a whole filo pastry sheet into $1/4$-inch strips. Very lightly spread the ghee on the sheets with a pastry brush. (You can also use some vegetable spray instead of ghee. Lightly spray the sheets with oil.) Stack four strips on top of each other. Place some of the chopped walnut mixture into the corner of the filo pastry. Fold into a triangle starting at the corner and keep folding until the triangle is complete. Place on a sprayed sheet pan and lightly brush some ghee on top and sprinkle with nutmeg. Bake at 350 degrees for 10 to 15 minutes, or until golden brown.

Appendix

For information on ongoing *Grow Younger, Live Longer* programs, log on to *www.chopra.com*.

Primordial Sound Meditation Teachers

To locate a certified Primordial Sound Meditation (PSM) teacher near you, log on to *www.chopra.com,* and go to: Find an Instructor in Your Area.

Recommended Relaxing and Inspiring Music

Becvar, B., and B. Becvar. *The Magic of Healing Music.* San Rafael, Calif.: Shining Star Productions, 1997.

Oldman, C. *Floating on Evening.* New Haven, Vt.: Coyote Oldman Music, 1998.

Coxon, R. H. *The Silent Path.* Quebec, Canada: R.H.C. Productions, 1995.

Evenson, D. *Ocean Dreams.* Tucson, Ariz.: Soundings of the Planet, 1989.

Raye, M. *Liquid Silk.* Penrose, Colo.: Native Heart Music, 1999.

Chopra, D. *A Gift of Love.* New York, N.Y.: Tommy Boy Music, 1998.

Sources of Products

The nutritional supplements described in this book are readily available from a wide range of sources, including health food stores and pharmacies. The Chopra Center Essentials line of nutrients has been designed to conform with the recommendations outlined in *Grow Younger, Live Longer.*

Visit *www.chopra.com* to access high-quality nutritional complements, herbs, and teas, including The Chopra Center Essentials, featuring amalaki jam (Chavanprash) available as Biochavan.

Our daily *Grow Younger, Live Longer* nutritional complement recommendations are:

1. A high-potency multivitamin (Chopra Center Daily Nutrients)
2. Calcium/magnesium/vitamin D tablets (Chopra Center Essentials—Bone Health Formula)
3. Menopause Formula or Men's Support Formula
4. One teaspoon of Biochavan or Biochavan wafer

We are pleased to announce The Grow Younger, Live Longer Fitness Program, a collaboration between The Chopra Center for Well Being and 24 Hour Fitness Worldwide. This program, exclusively available through 24 Hour Fitness, is specifically designed to maximize the age-reversing benefits of a balanced exercise program.

24 Hour Fitness, the world's largest fitness chain, has more than 430 centers in eleven countries. Their professional fitness staff is trained to create personalized fitness programs for people regardless of age, fitness level, or ability. To learn more about The Grow Younger, Live Longer Fitness Program at a 24 Hour Fitness Center in your area and receive a free guest pass to a facility near you, log on to: www.24HourFitness.com.

References

Chapter 1
Escaping the Prison of Conditioning

Langer, Ellen. *Mindfulness.* Reading, Mass.: Perseus Books, 1989.

Leaf, Alexander. *Youth in Old Age.* New York: McGraw-Hill, 1975.

Chapter 2
Changing Your Perceptions

Grey, Alex. *Sacred Mirrors: The Visionary Art of Alex Grey.* Rochester, Vt.: Inner Traditions International, 1990.

Murchie, Guy. *The Seven Mysteries of Life.* Boston: Houghton Mifflin, 1978, pp. 321–22.

Chapter 3
Restful Awareness and Restful Sleep

Stress

Cannon, Walter. Voodoo death. *American Anthropologist* 44(1943):168–81.

Selye, Hans. *The Stress of Life.* New York: McGraw-Hill, 1978.

Meditation

Elson, B. D.; P. Hauri; and D. Cunis. Physiological changes in yoga meditation. *Psychophysiology* 14(1977):52–57.

Ghista, D. N.; D. Nandagopal; et al. Physiological characterization of the "meditative state" during intuitional practice (the Ananda Marga system of meditation) and its therapeutic value. *Medical and Biological Engineering* 14(1976):209–13.

Glaser, J. L.; J. L. Brind; et al. Elevated serum dehydroepiandrosterone sulfate levels in practitioners of the Transcendental Meditation (TM) and TM-Sidhi programs. *Journal of Behavioral Medicine* 15(1992):327–41.

Wallace, R. K. Physiological effects of transcendental meditation. *Science* 167, no. 926 (1970):1751–54.

Wallace, R. K.; M. Dillbeck; et al. The effects of the transcendental meditation and TM-Sidhi program on the aging process. *International Journal of Neuroscience* 16(1982):53–58.

Sleep

Chopra, D. *Restful Sleep.* New York: Harmony Books, 1994.

Czeisler, C. A.; and E. B. Klerman. Circadian and sleep-dependent hormone release in humans. *Recent Progress in Hormone Research* 54(1999):97-130; discussion 130–32.

Irwin, M.; A. Mascovich; et al. Partial sleep deprivation reduces natural killer cell activity in humans. *Psychosomatic Medicine* 56(1994):493–98.

Shochat, T.; J. Umphress; et al. Insomnia in primary care patients. *Sleep* 22, Suppl. 2 (1999):S359–65.

Chapter 4
Nurturing Your Body Through Healthy Food

Key, Tj; G. K. Davey; and P. N. Appleby. Health benefits of a vegetarian diet. *Proceedings of the Nutrition Society* 58(1999):271–75.

Segasothy, M., and P. A. Phillips. Vegetarian diet: panacea for modern lifestyle diseases? *Quarterly Journal of Medicine* 92(1992):531–44.

Walter, P. Effects of vegetarian diets on aging and longevity. *Nutrition Reviews* 55, no. 1 Pt 2 (1997):S61–S65; discussion S65–S68.

Chapter 5
Using Nutritional Complements Wisely

For readers interested in the scientific basis of our nutritional complement recommendations, a detailed reference list is provided below.

Bauliey, E.; G. Thomas; et al. Dehdroepiandrosterone (DHEA), DHEA sulfate, and aging:

contribution of the DHEAge Study to a sociobiomedical issue. *Proceedings of the National Academy of Sciences* 97(2000):4279–84.

Bell, K. M.; S. G. Potkin; et al. S-adenosylmethionine blood levels in major depression: changes with drug treatment. *Acta Neurologica Scandinavica Supplementum* 154(1994):15–18.

Bressa, G. M. S-adenosyl-l-methanonine (SAMe) as antidepressant: meta-analysis of clinical studies. *Acta Neurologica Scandinavica Supplementum* 154(1994):7–14.

Cohn, L.; A. G. Feller; et al. Carpal tunnel syndrome and gynaecomastia during growth hormone treatment of elderly men with low circulating IGF-I concentrations. *Clinical Endocrinology* 39(1993):417–25.

Crook, T. H.; J. Tinklenberg; et al. Effects of phosphatidylserine in age-associated memory impairment. *Neurology* 41(1991):644–49.

Emmert, D. H., and J. T. Kirchner. The role of vitamin E in the prevention of heart disease. *Archives of Family Medicine* 8(1999):537–42.

Fine, A. M. Oligomeric proanthocyanidins complexes: history, structure, and phytopharmaceutical applications. *Alternative Medicine Review* 5(2000):144–51.

Glaser, J. L.; J. L. Brind; et al. Elevated serum dehyroepiandrosterone sulfate levels in practitioners of transcendental meditation TM and TM-Sidhi programs. *Journal of Behavioral Medicine* 15(1992):327–41.

Grimble, R. E., and P. S. Tappia. Modulation of pro-inflammatory cytokine biology by unsaturated fatty acids. *Zeitschrift für Ernährungswissenschaft* 37 Suppl. 1(1998):57–65.

Head, K. A. Ascorbic acid in the prevention and treatment of cancer. *Alternative Medicine Review* 3(1998):174–86.

Huppert, F. A.; J. K. Van Niekerk; and J. Herbert. Dehydroepiandrosterone (DHEA) supplementation for cognition and well-being. *The Cochrane Database of Systematic Reviews* 2(2000):CD000304.

Kroboth, P.; S. Firoozeh; et al. DHEA and DHEA-S: A Review. *Journal of Clinical Pharmacology* 39(1999):327–48.

Langsjoen, P. H., and A. M. Langsjoen. Overview of the use of CoQ10 in cardiovascular disease. *Biofactors* 9(1999):273–84.

McAlindon, T. E.; P. Jacques; et al. Do antioxidant micronutrients protect against the development and progression of knee osteoarthritis? *Arthritis and Rheumatology* 39(1996):648–56.

McAlindon, T. E.; M. P. La Valley; et al. Glucosamine and chondroitan for treatment of osteoarthritis: a systematic quality assessment and meta-analysis. *Journal of the American Medical Association* 283(2000):1469–75.

Marcell, T. J.; D. R. Taaffe; et al. Oral arginine does not stimulate basal or augment exercise-induced GH secretion in either young or old adults. *Journal of Gerontology. Series A, Biological Sciences and Medical Sciences* 54(1999):M395–99.

Martin-Du Pan, R. C. Are the hormones of youth carcinogenic? *Annales d'Endocrinologie* (Ann Endocrinol [Paris]) 60(1999):392–97.

Meydani, S. N.; M. Meydani; et al. Vitamin E supplementation and in vivo immune response in healthy elderly subjects. *Journal of the American Medical Association* 277(1997):1380–86.

Papadakis, M. A.; D. Grady; et al. Growth hormone replacement in healthy older men improves body composition but not functional ability. *Annals of Internal Medicine* 124(1996):708–16.

Perkins, A. J.; H. C. Hendrie; et al. Association of antioxidants with memory in a multiethnic elderly sample using the Third National Health and Nutrition Examination Survey. *American Journal of Epidemiology* 150(1999):37–44.

Pryor, W. A.; W. Stahl; and C. L. Rock. Beta-carotene: from biochemistry to clinical trials. *Nutrition Reviews* 58(2000):39–53.

Richardson, J. S. Neuroprotective agents. *Physical Medicine and Rehabilitation Clinics of North America* 10(1999):447–61.

Rigney, U.; S. Kimber; and I. Hindmarch. The effects of acute doses of standardized Ginkgo biloba extract on memory and psychomotor performance in volunteers. *Phytotherapy Research* 13(1999):408–15.

Rimm, E. B., and M. J. Stampfer. Antioxidants for vascular disease. *Medical Clinics of North America* 84(2000):239–49.

Rudman, D.; A. G. Feller; et al. Effects of human growth hormone in men over 60 years old. *New England Journal of Medicine* 323(1990):1–6.

Salvioli, G., and M. Neri. L-acetylcarnitine treatment of mental decline in the elderly. *Drugs under Experimental and Clinical Research* 20(1994):169–76.

Seshadri, N., and K. Robinson. Homocysteine, B vitamins, and coronary artery disease. *Medical Clinics of North America* 84(2000):215–37.

Shklar, G., and O. Se-Kying. Experimental basis for cancer prevention by vitamin E. *Cancer Investigation* 18(2000):214–22.

Thal, L. J.; A. Carta; et al. A one-year multicenter placebo-controlled study of acetyl-L-carnitine in patients with Alzheimer's disease. *Neurology* 47(1996):705–11.

Yarasheski, K. E.; J. J. Sachwieja; et al. Effect of growth hormone and resistance exercise on muscle growth and strength in older men. *American Journal of Physiology* 268, no. 2 pt 1 (1995):E268–76.

Chapter 6
Enhancing Mind/Body Integration

Garfinkel, M., and H. R. Schumacher, Jr. Yoga. *Rheumatic Diseases Clinics of North America* 26(2000):125–32.

Garfinkel, M. S.; A. Singhal; et al. Yoga-based intervention for carpal tunnel syndrome: a randomized trial. *Journal of the American Medical Association* 280(1998):1601–3.

Hong, Y.; J. X. Li; and P. D. Robinson. Balance control, flexibility and cardiorespiratory fitness among older Tai chi practitioners. *British Journal of Sports Medicine* 34(2000):29–34.

Jain, S. C.; A. Uppal; et al. A study of response pattern of non-insulin dependent diabetics to yoga therapy. *Diabetes Research and Clinical Practice* 19(1993):69–74.

Khanam, A. A.; U. Sachdeva; et al. Study of pulmonary and autonomic functions of asthma patients after yoga training. *Indian Journal of Physiology and Pharmacology* 40(1996):318–24.

Mayer, M. Qigong and hypertension: a critique of research. *Journal of Alternative and Complementary Medicine* 5(1999):371–82.

Pandya, D. P.; V. H. Vyas; and S. H. Vyas. Mind-body therapy in the management and prevention of coronary disease. *Comprehensive Therapy* 25(1999):283–93.

Wolf, S. L.; H. X. Barnhart; N. G. Kutner; et al. Reducing frailty and falls in older persons: an investigation of Tai Chi and computerized balance training. Atlanta FICSIT Group. Frailty and Injuries: Cooperative Studies of Intervention Techniques. *Journal of the American Geriatric Society* 44(1996):489–97.

Xu, S. H. Psychophysiological reactions associated with qigong therapy. *Chinese Medical Journal* (English) 107(1994):230–33.

Chapter 7
Exercise

Carpenter, D. M., and B. W. Nelson. Low back strengthening for the prevention and treatment of low back pain. *Medicine and Science in Sports and Exercise* 31(1999):18-24.

Douillard, J. *Body, Mind and Sport*. New York: Random House, 1994.

Evans, W., and I. H. Rosenberg. *Biomarkers—The 10 Determinants of Aging You Can Control.* New York: Simon & Schuster, 1992.

Fox, K. R. The influence of physical activity on mental well-being. *Public Health Nutrition* 2(1999):411–18.

Hassmen, P.; N. Koivula; and A. Uutela. Physical exercise and psychological well-being: a population study in Finland. *Preventive Medicine* 30(2000):17–35.

Kokkinos, P. F., and V. Papademetriou. Exercise and hypertension. *Coronary Artery Disease* 11(2000):99–102.

Messier, S. P.; T. D. Royer; et al. Long-term exercise and its effect on balance in older, osteoarthritic adults: results from the Fitness, Arthritis, and Seniors Trial (FAST). *Journal of the American Geriatric Society* 48(2000):131–38.

Miller, T. D.; G. J. Balady; and G. F. Fletcher. Exercise and its role in the prevention and rehabilitation of cardiovascular disease. *Annals of Behavioral Medicine* 19(1997):220–29.

Roberts, J. M., and K. Wilson. Effect of stretching duration on active and passive range of motion in the lower extremity. *British Journal of Sports Medicine* 33(1999):259–63.

Rockhill, B.; W. C. Willett; et al. A prospective study of recreational physical activity and breast cancer risk. *Archives of Internal Medicine* 25;159(1999):2290–96.

Saltin, B.; J. H. Blomqvist; et al. Responses to exercise after bed rest and after training. *Circulation* 38, supplement 7 (1968):VII-1 to VII-78.

Ulrich, C. M.; C. C. Georgiou; et al. Lifetime physical activity is associated with bone mineral density in premenopausal women. *Journal of Women's Health* 8(1999):365–75.

Chapter 8
Eliminating Toxins from Your Life

Batmanghelidj, F. *Your Body's Many Cries for Water.* Falls Church, Va.: Global Health Solutions, 1997.

Mack, G. W.; C. A. Weseman; et al. Body fluid balance in dehydrated healthy older men: thirst and renal osmoregulation. *Journal of Applied Physiology* 76(1994):1615–23.

Raichur, P. *Absolute Beauty.* New York: HarperPerennial, 1997.

Rosenberg, M. B. *Nonviolent Communication.* Del Mar, Calif.: Puddle-Dancer Press, 1999.

Sachs, M. *Ayurvedic Beauty Care.* Twin Lakes, Wis.: Lotus Press, 1994.

Stookey, J. D. The diuretic effects of alcohol and caffeine and total water intake misclassification. *European Journal of Epidemiology* 15(1999):181–88.

Stout, N. R.; R. A. Kenny; and P. H. Baylis. A review of water balance in aging in health and disease. *Gerontology* 45(1999):61–66.

Chapter 9
Cultivating Flexibility and Creativity in Consciousness

Course in Miracles, A. Tiburon, Calif.: Foundation for Inner Peace, 1975.

Easwaran, Eknath. *Dialogue With Death.* Tomales, Calif.: Nilgiri Press, 1998.

Goswami, Amit. *Quantum Creativity.* Cresskill, N.J.: Hampton Press, 1999.

Chapter 10
Love

Agarwal, R.; S. Diwanay; et al. Studies on immunomodulatory activity of Withania somnifera (Ashwagandha) extracts in experimental immune inflammation. *Journal of Ethnopharmacology* 67(1999):27–35.

Al-Qarawi, A. A.; H. A. Abdel-Rahman; et al. The effect of extracts of cynomorium coccineum and withania somnifera on gonadotrophins and ovarian follicles of immature wistar rats. *Phytotherapy Research* 14(2000):288–90.

Brecher, E. M. *Love, Sex and Ageing. Consumer's Union report.* Boston: Little, Brown, 1984.

Choi, Y. D.; R. H. Rha; and H. K. Choi. In vitro and in vivo experimental effect of Korean red ginseng on erection. *Journal of Urology* 162(1999):1508–11.

Deepak and friend: *A Gift of Love.* New York: Tommy Boy Music, 1998.

Frasure-Smith, N., and R. Prince. The ischemic heart disease life stress monitoring program: impact on mortality. *Psychosomatic Medicine* 47(1985):431–45.

McClelland, D. C. The effect of motivational arousal through films on salivary immunoglobulin A. *Psychology and Health* 2(1988):31–52.

Medalie, J. H., and U. Goldbourt. Angina pectoris among 10,000 men. II. Psychosocial and other risk factors as evidenced by a multivariate analysis of a five-year incidence study. *American Journal of Medicine* 60(1976):910–21.

Nerem, R. M.; M. J. Levesque; and J. F. Cornhill. Social environment as a factor in diet-induced atherosclerosis. *Science* 1980; 208(1980):1475–76.

Sharma, S.; S. Ramji; et al. Randomized controlled trial of Asparagus racemosus (Shatavari) as a lactogogue in lactational inadequacy. *Indian Pediatrics.* 33(1996):675–77.

Simon, D., and D. Chopra. *The Chopra Center Herbal Handbook—Forty Natural Prescriptions for Perfect Health*. New York: Three Rivers Press, 2000. For more information on ashwagandha, shatavari, and amalaki.

Spiegel, D.; J. R. Bloom; et al. Effect of psychosocial treatment on survival of patients with metastatic breast cancer. *Lancet* 2(1989):888–91.

Chapter 11
Maintaining a Youthful Mind

Kamei, T.; H. Kumano; and S. Masumura. Changes of immunoregulatory cells associated with psychological stress and humor. *Perceptual and Motor Skills* 84(1997):1296–98.

Ladinsky, D. *I Heard God Laughing—Renderings of Hafiz*. Walnut Creek, Calif.: Sufism Reoriented, 1996.

Maslow, A. H.; R. Frager; and J. Fadiman. *Motivation and Personality.* Boston: Addison-Wesley Pub. Co., 1997.

Richman, J. The lifesaving function of humor with the depressed and suicidal elderly. *Gerontologist* 35(1995):271–73.

Epilogue

Hilton, J. *Lost Horizon.* New York: Pocket Books/Simon & Schuster, 1933, 1960.

Osho. *The Book of Secrets.* New York: St. Martin's Griffin, 1974.

Index

A

B

C

F

G

H

I

N

O

P

Q

S

V

W

Y

About the Authors

More than a decade ago, DEEPAK CHOPRA, M.D., founder of the Chopra Center for Well Being in La Jolla, California, became the foremost pioneer in integrated medicine. His insights have redefined our vision of health to embrace body, mind, and spirit. His books, which include *Quantum Healing; Perfect Health; Ageless Body, Timeless Mind;* and *The Seven Spiritual Laws of Success,* have become international bestsellers and established classics of their kind.

DAVID SIMON, M.D., a graduate of the University of Chicago Medical School, is a neurologist and an expert in Ayurveda, the traditional medical system that has its roots in ancient India. His earlier books include *The Wisdom of Healing, Return to Wholeness, Vital Energy,* and the *Chopra Center Herbal Handbook.* He is cofounder of the Chopra Center for Well Being, where he serves as its medical director.